I believe the world would be a better place if everyone could hear Jason's story.

—Jana Waller, Host, *Skull Bound TV*

Jason Koger is the embodiment of relentless determination and in hearing his story, at the very least you will be afforded the opportunity to reflect on how fortunate you are in your own life, which is something we all need to do right now. Jason's story is one of fortitude, resilience, and sacrifice. When you actually meet the man and hear his story, it's impossible not to be inspired.

—Alex O'Loughlin, actor, *Hawaii Five-0*

Jason has returned from near death and an excruciating setback as an amputee to become one of the most positive and motivational human beings whom I know. For the very purpose of human perseverance, tenacity, and dignity, Jason's story is vibrant with anyone and all of us for our moments of doubt and shadow. We *can* overcome anything.

—Dr. Peter Weller, actor, director

We all need to be reminded to think positive and that no matter how bad things are, someone has it worse and honestly things will get better. Jason's story is truly inspiring and it makes me proud to know him and be his friend.

—Travis "T-Bone" Turner, co-host, *Bone Collector* and *Realtree Road Trips*; National Spokesperson, Whitetails Unlimited

When I think of Jason, two words come to mind: inspiration and perseverance. Jason is a wonderful person with an uplifting attitude. His message is that no matter what difficult situations you come against in life, you can persevere. Jason is the epitome of overcoming difficulties and persevering through hard work.

—Mark McManus, General President, United Association of Plumbers, Pipefitters, and Sprinkler Fitters

Jason is a one-of-a-kind guy who exudes joy and a lust for life that is undeniable. Jason has turned the life-changing event of losing his arms into one of incredible "true grit" and inspiration. Not only is he an amazing gift to other individuals who have lost one or both arms, but he inspires some of the most seasoned professionals, like me, in ways that are hard to describe.

—Professor Diane J. Atkins, OTR, FISPO,
Baylor College of Medicine

There is no one better to come speak to your group or company than Jason Koger! I am so thankful for his friendship and out of all the individual people I know there is no better person than Jason.

—Timothy "TK" Klund, entrepreneur, author, corporate speaker

Jason makes an impact in everything he does and with everything he says. By sharing his story and giving back the way he does, Jason has saved more lives than any of us will ever know.

—Jared Ashley, musician, founder of Operation Cherrybend

Jason's story needs to be told and whoever doesn't already know it needs to hear it. I hope you read every word, and I hope his words inspire you the way they inspired me. We've all been through something. And we've all got a story. But whatever it is you've been through, I hope reading this book and meeting my buddy Jason helps you find a new mission and a greater purpose too.

—Ted DiBiase, Jr., former WWE champion, actor, businessman

HANDED *a* GREATER PURPOSE

JASON KOGER

**WITH DANNY MAY
AND KAREN HUNSANGER**

Cover design by Tanner+West
tannerwest.com

Book design by Eric Butler

ISBN 978-1-953058-51-5

Printed in the United States of America

Published by
Butler Books
www.butlerbooks.com

CONTENTS

Photo courtesy of Advanced Arm Dynamics

INTRODUCTION

November 8, 2019

Not a day goes by where I don't think, *Is this really my life?* Especially as I'm about to step on stage or walk to the podium to tell my story in front of hundreds or thousands of people.

It's not that I get nervous. I don't. Not really. It's just that I never, ever dreamed in a million years I'd be a motivational speaker and show others what is possible with faith, attitude, and family.

One of the first things I always tell people is the only class I ever failed was public speaking. Which got a pretty good chuckle as the moderator introduced me at my first TEDx talk.

I was standing just offstage behind the curtain, taking a deep breath and soaking it all in, excited to get my chance onstage after listening to the other awesome speakers that night. Then, as I heard my name, I stepped out from behind the curtain and into the bright stage lights.

The first thing that struck me was how dark it is on a TEDx stage. I couldn't see much of anything beyond the red circle carpet they told us to stand on. As I turned toward the crowd, the TEDx logo was just behind me, off to the right. Directly behind me was a large, LED screen with my name on it to serve as a backdrop. A stool with a bottle of water stood just to my left. I knew somewhere at the foot of the stage was a timer and out in the crowd there were lots of faces staring back at me; I just couldn't see them. I'm used to speaking at school assemblies in gyms, or church sanctuaries, or conference settings. This was much more intimate, but it felt huge because I knew there were going to be countless more faces watching this online.

I also knew it was likely that I already had the attention of all of those people. At least at first. One advantage of being a bilateral upper arm amputee is that most people don't see a guy with bionic hands every day, so all I really have to do is walk on stage and it's all eyes on me. Or my arms, I should say.

The same thing happens in restaurants, or Walmart, or wherever. Especially if I'm wearing a T-shirt where people can see the carbon fiber sockets and devices I am wearing. My socket, which is what you might call my forearm part, has pictures of my family all over it, which is pretty cool. Since I sometimes wear hooks, I've gotten used to stares over the years.

At something like a TEDx talk, I use that immediate attention to my advantage. The trick is keeping people engaged after they get used to seeing my bionic hands. But that night, I was ready. I had worked with my coaches. I had prepared and practiced at home. I felt good about my talk and I was excited to get a chance to share my story on a platform as popular as TEDx.

The thing I wasn't sure about was the timing. I'm used to telling my story in 30 or 45 minutes. Sometimes more. It's actually easier for me to tell my story in an hour than it is in 20 minutes. But a TEDx talk is a different format. They give you 15-18 minutes to share your "idea worth spreading." I was invited to speak on the topic, "Why just survive when you can thrive?"

My opening went great! I wore my bionic hands like I always do when I give talks. They're a little dressier than my body-powered hooks when I go out in public. On my left arm I wore my myoelectric ETD hook from Fillauer. On my right, I wore an i-Limb Quantum from Össur, which is the most advanced bionic hand in the world. Both have a built-in wrist rotator. The crowd clapped when I held my right arm up and spun my wrist completely around 360 degrees. Yeah, there's an app for that, too!

They also laughed when I held up my two favorite T-shirts: "Look Ma, No Hands!" and "Don't Shoot! I'm Unarmed." Then I hit the highlights of my story that I've given hundreds of times over the past several years.

My best entrance, though, was the time my buddy Reggie Showers and I rode a double-seated bicycle and filmed it. That got a good laugh too when we showed it on the big screen at the first "Handing Back" fundraising event here in Owensboro, Kentucky. He's an amputee who lost both his legs in an electrical accident. I rode on the front seat and he rode on the back seat. The visual was a guy with no arms holding the handlebars for a guy with no legs pedaling this wobbly bike down the banks of the Ohio River.

During my talks I don't go into specific details about my accident. I don't have time to tell the full story of my recovery and all the ways the Lord has blessed me since. This book gives me the chance to do that.

With this book I hope to thank my family, friends, and community for standing by me and supporting me.

I hope to encourage people going through a hard time, especially other amputees.

And I hope to inspire people that prayer and a positive attitude can change any situation because God works *all things* for the good of those who love him.

These pages will give me a chance to tell the whole story in a way that I can't in 20 minutes, or even an hour.

It will also give me the chance to explain some things and answer some questions people have asked me over the years. For instance, what it's like to be a bilateral arm amputee. How I'm still able to hunt and do the things I love, like mow the yard and play catch with my kids. Things like that.

For years, people have been telling me I should write a book. I always thought I would one of these days. This book is another chance to help others in a positive way and give all the glory to God. What happened to me wasn't a punishment; it was a gift. When the whole world shut down for the coronavirus and several months' worth of bookings got canceled, it gave me time to focus on the book and get it down on paper.

The COVID-19 quarantine was a great time to think back on all that's happened in the past 14 years since my accident. Putting this book together has really been a great reminder to me of how the Lord has blessed us, and continues to.

There were some really funny quarantine moments. Like the time my wife, Jenny, sent me to the store to buy some essential items before things went really crazy. Here I am, a guy with no hands, buying hand sanitizer. The lady at the checkout counter didn't know what to think! That got some good laughs when I posted it on Facebook later that night.

But there were so many great moments at home with Jenny and the kids, just being together, hanging out around the house. Sometimes we went hunting or fishing in the morning on what would have been a school day. One day I posted a picture of my son Axell and me outside painting a swing set together that I had to use a grinder to get all the old, chipped paint off of. I posted a video of how I use a grinder with my body-powered prostheses. That led to people asking how I do other things. Then I posted additional videos of little everyday things like how I open a carton of milk, how I do the dishes, and other things around the house.

People are curious about things like that, which I totally

understand. This whole situation is really amazing when you stop and think about it.

Here's a quick example. Have you ever really stopped to consider how intricate the human brain is? Or how much information goes from the tips of your fingers up to your brain when you slip your hand in your pocket.

Probably not.

But think about it for just one second.

Isn't it astounding that you can pick a needle up off the floor? Think about trying that with hooks for hands.

See what I mean?

Those are the little, everyday things that I used to take for granted that just blow my mind now as an amputee. It amazes me now how when you stick your hands in your pocket your brain can tell the difference between a penny, a nickel, a dime, or a quarter simply from those little nuances of size and texture. Your fingertips send so much information to your brain it's unbelievable. You realize that so much more when you lose your hands.

When I reach into my pocket for something now, I can't jiggle around between my car keys and find a certain coin or piece of gum or whatever else I might need like I used to. Before I lost my hands, I could have felt my way around those coins, grabbed that piece of gum instead, still had a full conversation with someone, unwrapped it, stuck it in my mouth, and thrown away the wrapper without even looking at it. I could have still kept eye contact with that person the whole time too.

But now, I have to pull everything out of my pocket one thing at a time until I actually have that piece of gum. Then I need to lay it down somewhere and put my full attention on it. I have to think it through step by step to unwrap that stupid thing one corner at a time, which is a lot easier if I have my hooks on, but I can do it with my bionic hands if I need to.

Or I'll reach down into my pocket as deep as I can, grab the lining at the bottom of my pocket, pull it inside out, and dump everything in my pocket out on a counter or table all at once. Someone with real hands would never do that. But that's the easiest way for me.

You, as a person who still has your hands, would never tell yourself, "Stop. You've got a hold of your pants pocket. Let go of that and just grab your keys." You never have those thoughts.

I, on the other hand (sorry! I couldn't resist!), I'm thinking to myself, "Yes! I got my pocket liner on the first try. I'm getting really good at this."

I'm getting to the point now that I can almost tell the difference between certain things when I reach in my pocket, but that took a long time.

After my accident, my daughter Billie Grace would dig the change out of my pockets for me. Or I'd walk in the house and she'd reach in my pockets and put my keys and wallet and any loose change on the counter. It just became our thing. She did that for years. When Axell was old enough, he started doing that too. But with Axell, he would always keep my change and go run to his room and drop it in his piggy bank. He thought that was his way of earning money, I guess.

All in all, there aren't many things I was able to do before that I haven't figured out how to do now with my prostheses. It's just way different and in some situations, it takes me a little longer, but I've learned to be patient with myself. It took years of hard work, practice, getting the right fit for my sockets, and having good equipment to work with.

My success has definitely been a team effort. As you'll hear more later, I wouldn't be where I am today if it wasn't for the help and support of my amazing wife who has always been right by my side, and my family who was always supportive, no matter what. Then there were the people of Owensboro who supported all of us in so many ways. But most important is my faith in God, and my ability to maintain a positive attitude. Faith was extremely important early on after my accident, so I always say that faith is what got me through. But hearing the footsteps of my kids when they got out of bed every morning is also what motivated me. Billie, Cambell, and Axell have been my inspiration.

That was the message I gave that night at my first TEDx talk and it's the same message I give any time I have the opportunity to share my story.

So here it is, for you, in much more detail. There's a lot to tell, so thank you for taking the time. I hope it helps you consider your own story, and I hope it helps you think about how God is at work in your life too.

As you read you will have an opportunity to meet some of the people who were important in my life throughout my experience. I've invited some others who were a major part of my story to share their perspective as we go. While they were being interviewed for this book, I asked them to also share some insight about other parts of my story besides my accident and recovery. It's amazing that 14 years after my accident, I still learned so much by hearing the things they've shared for this book.

Looking back, I truly was in the grip of grace the day that everything changed, and I have been every day since.

In fact, I think we all are, whether we realize it or not.

Here is my story.

THE MOMENT THAT CHANGED EVERYTHING

"I knew I had to do something. What would you do?"
~JASON

I've always been told that if you're on rubber tires, like I was, then electricity won't shock you.

That was the very first thought that flashed through my head as I was trying to process the fact that I had just come into direct contact with a downed power line while riding on my four-wheeler.

It was just like time stopped. But it also felt like an eternity. I remember the sound of complete silence, like a slow-motion

Photo courtesy of Advanced Arm Dynamics

movie scene, even though the motor was still running. I felt the line resting heavy across both forearms as I still gripped the handlebars, but my brain couldn't make any sense of what my eyes were seeing. I didn't notice the low-hanging power line until I had completely run up under it.

Immediately, I let off the throttle and slammed on the brake so the four-wheeler came to a stop. Now here I was, frozen in fear and panic with the power line still draped across both arms while the four-wheeler sat idling.

It's amazing how in a moment like that a thousand thoughts pass through your mind in a split second. I remember thinking I wasn't electrocuted, but I totally expected to be in the very next moment. It was surreal.

I didn't know what to do or how to react. But I knew I had to do something.

What should I do?

What would *you* do?

I remember thinking that since I wasn't shocked immediately, and since that line ran down to the pump house out in the lower field, then that must mean the power was shut off because it didn't do anything to me.

Or was it really because I was sitting on four tires?

Should I just raise it up with one hand and drive under it?

Should I back away slowly and carefully?

Or should I back up as fast as I can and get the heck out of there?

Those were some of the questions that were flashing through my mind. But it wasn't the initial contact with that downed power line that caused the injury that changed my life forever.

It was what happened next . . .

CHAPTER 2

GROWING UP

*"People ask me all the time how I can keep such a
positive attitude with what I've gone through. I say
two things: my faith in God, and how I was raised."*
~JASON

I can see now that certain things in my upbringing prepared me
for what happened to me. I didn't notice it then, but I can look
back and see how hard my parents worked, and how faithful they
were.

My dad started his business with almost nothing and built
a successful company on hard work. I watched him work long
hours and put his heart and soul into his work and family. He
was a drill sergeant in the army. He was very disciplined and had
that military work ethic. If he wanted to reach a goal, he worked
to get there.

My mom was a hard worker too. She comes from a farming
family and they were all hard workers. She worked as a nurse
when we were growing up. Plus, she has always kept the books
and done the billing for the business they started together. She
was really good at running the office. While my dad was out
growing the business and wheeling and dealing, Mom was
handling all the business back at the workplace. In the beginning,
her nursing salary is what helped them get the business up and
running. Even today, my dad is the one in the public eye as a
county commissioner, but Mom supports him behind the scenes.

That team effort is what makes them work so well together and what I think has made their business so successful too.

Since my accident I can see how all of their hard work became the backbone of our family. I watched my mom and dad go from struggling as they were starting the business when I was young,

and now I see where they are today. I think watching them prepared me to overcome obstacles too.

A FOUNDATION OF FAITH

"I wonder if God was preparing him for what happened all those years later."
~DONNA KOGER

Faith was just a part of life for us growing up. I was raised going to church and I honestly can't say I ever had a time in life where I lost my faith. Not even when my accident happened. I never had a moment where I had to "wake up" or find God, because I have always believed in God and trusted in Him.

My story is not so much that God saved me from this tragedy and now I've seen the light. I do believe God saved my life that day, but I had faith way before then. I always believed. Maybe I appreciate my faith more now and I understand it a little deeper. But I was a Christian way before my accident.

I don't really have a first memory of church because we went every weekend. My mom and dad raised us in the Catholic faith and I was baptized as a baby, a few miles from home at St. Anthony Catholic Church in Browns Valley, Kentucky.

I remember it being a small country church. My grandparents got married there. My parents got married there. I've even heard stories about my grandparents riding a horse and buggy to church and how my mom grew up going there. I made my first communion in second grade and confirmation in eighth grade at St. Anthony.

I have never known what it was like not to believe. I can say that when I was young, prayers were a part of our daily routine.

When we got married, Jenny was Baptist and I was Catholic, so we had Jenny's preacher and a priest at our wedding together. I went to church with Jenny almost every weekend when we started dating. But I've always been the type of person that doesn't care much about denomination as long as you're going to church. When Jenny and I got married, we would go to both churches sometimes. Then we started going to Owensboro Christian for a while, which is nondenominational. But it felt huge to us because we were both used to worshiping in small churches.

Now we go to Pleasant Grove Baptist Church. We like it because they do a lot of ministries for kids, and that is important to us. We also wanted a smaller setting for our kids.

People ask me all the time if my accident was a spiritual turning point for me, but I really don't think it was because I already had that foundation. My faith was already a part of my life. Not so much because it was something I was taught or the fact that I was raised Catholic or belonged to a Baptist church when the accident happened, but because I just knew God had my back. I never doubted His existence, even in my worst time. It was more of a trust thing. I just knew the Lord would lead me down a path to overcome things. I can't even say I had a certain verse in the Bible that helped me through, like some people say they have. It was just knowing in my heart and soul that He would get me through this and we would be okay. I just knew.

I remember my mom telling me a story about when I was really sick as a kid. I was lying in bed with a high temperature. She came in to check on me and I was staring at the ceiling with a big smile on my face. She thought the fever might be causing me to see things. But when she checked my temperature, the fever was gone. My mom recalls the moment:

"I remember that night very vividly in my mind, it will stay with me forever. When I went to check on him, he was laying in his bed staring straight up at the ceiling. Suddenly he had the sweetest smile I've ever seen on a child. I went over to the bedside and put my hand on his forehead to feel for a fever and he said softly, 'I saw Jesus.'

"I said, 'What?' And he said it again. 'I saw Jesus. I waved at Him.' It gave me chills. He didn't feel like he had a fever, but I took his temperature anyway just to make sure and it was normal.

"I mentioned it the next day to our parish priest and he said he had no doubt in his mind that Jason had seen a vision.

"I've never forgotten it, but after his accident, I have thought about it even more and I wonder if God was preparing him for what happened all those years later.

"I truly believe whatever went on that night was the beginning of Jason's journey of God preparing him for all this now. I just feel that."

My dad helped to reinforce the strength of my faith when I was growing up too. He was a true believer and often told me the story about when he started believing in miracles. When my parents became engaged, my dad was Baptist but my mom had been raised Catholic. When they were married, he converted so they could be the same denomination. He felt in his heart that it was the right thing to do.

When he decided to become Catholic, he really liked the priest at St. Anthony. When he went through the instruction and it came time for his first confession the priest said they could sit in the booth behind a closed door. My dad said, "Well, if it's all right with you, can I just sit across the table?" The priest was fine with that so they just sat at the dining room table in the rectory and he took his time. It was nice and felt more comfortable.

At this point in time, he and my mom had been married about five years and they were trying to have a child. As he and the priest were finishing up, the priest asked if there was a certain thing my dad would like to pray about. Dad mentioned to him that he and my mom were trying to have a child but it hadn't happened yet and they didn't know why. They had all these tests done and still nothing. Dad told him if they could just pray about that he would appreciate it. So, they did. My dad describes that what happened next that changed his life forever.

"I told Donna afterward that at one special moment in that prayer I had this special feeling in my body. It was only a few days later and Donna was pregnant. I couldn't believe it! I still feel it was a miracle."

That was my sister Holly. Four years later they had me with no problem. My dad knew that he had experienced a miracle.

My dad says: "I told Father that it was a feeling that I had never felt before, nor have I felt it since. Up until today. It was that one special time. I can't explain it. But I believe that miracles can happen because for whatever reason that happened to me. I know what I felt."

As an adult, seeing so many little miracles helped to reinforce my faith too. Especially when our kids were born, seeing them being born was amazing. Not knowing you can love someone as much as you do. It's almost indescribable how much you love your kids. You don't even understand it's possible until you have your first child. When our girls were born, and later Axell, it really helped my faith grow and become more real. But like I said, it's always been there.

GIVING BACK

"Trying to teach Jason was interesting because he's like me, pretty soft-hearted. He's always been concerned about doing things for others. That's always been his personality."
~Mike Koger

I know that my parents both worked hard and sacrificed to get where they are now. One thing I think back on is how my dad worked a regular job and then built his business from scratch on the side until it was able to take off. He wasn't around at ballgames as much as I wished he could have been when Holly and I were younger. But I also realize now that my dad didn't have a lot growing up and he had to work hard from the time he was 13 to get ahead, and he did. Because of that, he wanted Holly and I to be able to have some things that he wasn't able to have when he was growing up. That was more important to him than being at all of our games. I'm glad for it now.

But that also plays into my dad's motivation for giving to others so much too. Like I said, my dad didn't have extra growing up, so once he and Mom were in a position to get a little ahead, they started giving to Christmas Wish and other charities as much as they could. They still give like that all the time, but nobody knows about it.

I remember being just a little boy and going along with Dad one time to deliver Christmas presents to another family. It made me realize that I got everything I wanted for Christmas, and probably more. It really hit me when I saw the homes those kids were living in. They were like my dad's situation when he was growing up. That was an eye-opener for me.

Holly and I grew up not wanting for anything because my parents worked hard and sacrificed for us. Because of that, they could bless others too.

They enjoyed that. We saw the joy they got from it. So, that's something else I picked up from my parents. It wasn't really ever taught as much as it was observed. Work hard. Be respectful. Give to others. Appreciate what you have. Share whatever you can.

My mom's family were big farmers. She had it a little more comfortable growing up than Dad did, but again, she picked up that hard work ethic too.

The stories I heard growing up about leaner times back then always made an impression on me as a kid. I remember my dad saying when we were little that his parents never owned anything, and the first thing my dad wanted to do when he got enough extra money was to buy his mom and dad a house to live in.

Today, I've seen my dad do things that people have no clue about. Which is the way he wants it. But he is a very, very giving and generous person. He'd much rather give someone else something than buy himself anything and I think that goes back to his upbringing. But I appreciate that about my mom and my dad because I think it's embedded in me and it's probably why I enjoy giving back too.

All of that has helped me be able to do what I do today. After my accident I had an opportunity to do an event in my hometown with actor Peter Weller. I really enjoy doing the "Handing Back" event and helping my community and other amputees any way I can. I want to do anything I can to help. But that all goes back to what I learned by watching Mom and Dad as I was growing up.

A STRONG WORK ETHIC

"Looking back, because I didn't think about it much at the time, I realize now that working early on, and teaching myself to do things, show my determination and curiosity. Those things paid off for me during my recovery after my accident."

~Jason

My sister Holly and I were brought up having to work hard for what we wanted. We even had to work for our first cars. They weren't just bought and given to us. We had to earn them. I appreciate that now. Dad didn't want to give us everything and have us not appreciate anything. I raised an acre or two of tobacco for several years in order to pay for my first truck.

Way before that little tobacco patch, I remember being a little boy, six or seven, sweeping floors in my dad's shop. My dad was a member of Union Local 633 Plumbers/Pipefitters and started Consolidated Mechanical in the early '80s. It started residential but by the time I began working for my dad as a teenager it had grown into commercial jobs. I enjoyed spending time with my dad. I wanted to be right there beside him and it's still like that today.

I also worked with my family on the farm a little bit in the summer, but I never did work full time because I worked for my dad.

Starting out, I did the jobs nobody else wanted to do. I was the gopher. Straightening up. Cleaning things. Putting things away. Then later I got to run equipment and drive a forklift. You can bet that anytime there was a job that meant somebody had to crawl under a house they called on me for that one!

Gradually I got to do more and more things as I got older. As soon as I was old enough, I used to get off the bus and drive to my dad's shop in town to go work a few hours after school.

I also taught myself how to drive a stick shift by watching my mom drive my dad's S-10 pickup. I'd watched how she shifted and listened to the motor change and tried to figure it out. One day I told my dad I wanted to learn and he said, "Okay, go drive it around the farm." I guess he thought I couldn't get it started and get it out of gear, but that's exactly what I did.

Looking back, those are the types of things I didn't think about much at the time, but I realize now that working early on, and teaching myself to do things, all show my determination and curiosity that paid off for me during my recovery after my accident.

I went to Atlanta a few weeks ago and was told that I'm one of the best prosthesis users in the world when it comes to functionality, based on some tests they ran. I showed up not knowing what I had to do, but the test was that I had to unpack a suitcase, fold everything nice and neat, take a big bottle of shampoo and fill a little travel bottle, put it into a Ziploc bag and seal it up, repack the suitcase, and zip it shut. The fastest time by other amputees at that point was 26 minutes. I did it in 19 minutes and said, "Hey, we've got time for a coffee break!" They were amazed.

My brain is just good at figuring things out. I'm just that determined. Always have been. I don't want to be "just okay" at anything I do. I want to be really good. That goes back to watching my dad doing what he wanted to do. I'm not bragging, by any means. That's just how our brains are wired, I guess. Just determined and willing to work hard to be successful.

I guess that's why I was always tinkering with something growing up. Building things for fun. Putting something together.

I enjoyed trying to figure out how things work. I'd put toys together myself and even put furniture together and things like that when I was a kid.

RACING

"What kid doesn't want to drive something fast?"
~JASON

When I was a little older, I got into racing cars and it was the same sort of deal; trying to figure out how to make the engine run better. Figuring out how to make it turn better in the corner and come out faster to adjusting the shocks and springs. I wanted to know how to get a little more speed than the other guy. I worked on the cars a lot myself but I also had tons of help from my buddy Matt Ebelhar.

Well, the way it worked out for me, my cousin was racing go-karts at the Daviess County Fairgrounds and my granddad let me run a go-kart with my cousin. It was fun. I loved the speed of it, and the challenge and competition of it.

When I turned 16, I told my dad I thought I'd like to race cars. My dad bought me an old car and I completely stripped it down with some of my buddies, did the body work on it, and got it ready to race. Me and my buddies would work on it after school and on the weekends. We built it up with new metal, painted it, striped it. We did everything but paint the number on the side.

My granddad loved racing but he was in a nursing home at the time. I kept it a secret from him that I was building that car but my plan was to tell him a few days before my first race and let him tell me what number he thought it should be. But he passed away before I had a chance to ask him, so instead I picked the number 84 because he was 84 years old when he died. I was fortunate to win the first race I ever raced in that car with #84 at Windy Hollow Speedway.

I guess racing on the weekends and working on cars at night kept us out of trouble. I was just a hobby racer, a weekend warrior as they say. I raced at Kentucky Lake Motor Speedway and sometimes out of state in Ohio or Tennessee.

We got to the point where we did all the body work ourselves. We'd start with a four-foot by eight-foot sheet of metal and bend it into the body shape we wanted using my dad's tools. We had a fast car, and we ran it almost every weekend.

One of my best friends, Matt Ebelhar, was very mechanically inclined. He helped me a lot because he is a very intelligent guy and smart when it comes to motors and anything automotive. We learned together and he was a huge part of my success because of the work he did on my cars.

When Matt and I first started talking about racing, we were still in high school. I was running go-karts at the time with my cousin when Matt and I started talking about building a car. There's no way I could have ever done all that by myself, so I have to credit Matt with really getting me started in racing. He loved working on the cars and really got me started.

When we raced, Matt and I made a good team. We learned a lot together about racing and making cars go faster. When I started racing late-model cars on dirt tracks, those engines were 780 horsepower and we could hit over 100mph on a three-eighths-mile track. I finally figured it out when somebody told me one time that when you go into a corner in a dirt late model you have to be on the gas hard until you see God. In other words, until you think you're going to die. And then once you see God, hold it in another two seconds and then let up. That's what you had to do to make it turn right through a curve. You'd feel like you were flying into the curve and you were going to lose it and end up in a wall if you didn't get in the throttle just right.

Matt would set my car up exactly right and have it dialed in a certain way and then he'd tell me exactly when and how to hit the throttle right for the turns. I trusted him. He'd tell me when to go in harder and when to come out of it. I would do exactly what he said and it would turn just like we wanted it to. If he told me to go in wide open, I knew I could do it because he knew exactly what we could get out of the car. It was amazing. It was so much fun. I loved racing!

I had no way of knowing what would happen to me later. But I am telling you about my earlier experiences because, looking back, I truly believe that working in the shop with my dad, working on the farm with my uncles, and tinkering on those race cars with Matt really helped me to be able to adapt to prostheses so well later on. It was figuring things out, breaking them down, seeing how things worked, and finding ways to do it better. That's always been how my mind works.

HUNTING

"I have a picture of me as a kid in the back of a red pickup truck with three deer in it."
~JASON

Hunting was my other hobby. My great-uncle hunted. He was my dad's mom's brother and he had a farm in Greenville, Kentucky where he raised cattle.

We'd go over there when I was a kid and spend time on the farm and hang out with him. One day he told my dad, "Why don't you bring Jason down here and let him go deer hunting with me." I went deer hunting with him a couple times and I just loved it from the start. He taught me everything I know about hunting. I tried to take my dad once but he said, "It's too cold, man!"

I was nine or 10 when my uncle got me started hunting. I'd spend the whole weekend with him and we'd hunt each morning.

My neighbor took me squirrel hunting a few times, too. I like to go once or twice a year and that's about it. Same with rabbit hunting and fishing. I never got into that much, either. There are so many rabbits on the farm out here there's not much challenge to it. I might take Axell every now and then, but that's about it.

Deer and turkey hunting is still what I love.

THIS IS MY TOWN

"Owensboro is just a big small town, and that's what I like about it."

~JASON

When people I meet on the road ask me where I'm from, I love to tell them about Owensboro, Kentucky. But mainly I tell them about the people and how this entire community supported me and my family so much after my accident. The outpouring this community had was just incredible, and people are impressed by it when I tell them about it.

Let me try and show you around town a little bit.

Any visit to Owensboro usually starts with a trip to the riverfront. We don't have a town square, but our Riverwalk along the Ohio River is really the main attraction of our downtown district.

Owensboro sits right along a little horseshoe bend in the river where the "blue bridge," as we call it, crosses from Indiana into Owensboro.

OWENSBORO RIVERFRONT

If you've never seen the Ohio River, it's a big one. I'd say it's almost a mile across looking over to the Indiana bank from our Kentucky side. The water moves fast from the east to the southwest, until it meets the Mississippi River and flows down to New Orleans. Barges float by all day long. A lot of lazy fishing boats and pontoons. In the summertime you might see a water-skier behind a speedboat, or a Jet Ski crisscrossing the ripples behind a barge. The boat ramp is downriver and always has a line of trucks with empty trailers that have dropped their boats for the day.

Owensboro is a small city of about 60,000 people. If you look at a map, you'll find our tiny dot about two hours downriver from Louisville and about 45 minutes upriver from Evansville, Indiana.

The Blue Bridge is the iconic backdrop to our downtown riverfront, which is only a few blocks long. Over the years while I was growing up, the riverfront grew too. Once it was a small setting with only a boat ramp, gazebo, fountain, and a swing set. Now it has a fine-arts center called the RiverPark Center where concerts, off-Broadway shows. and the symphony perform. For twenty years now the RiverPark Center has put up an outdoor stage for a summer street festival series called "Friday After Five" that thousands of people show up to each week.

Owensboro Convention Center was part of a huge renovation project that included two hotels overlooking the river. The mile or so in between the Convention Center and the RiverPark Center has all been redeveloped in phases.

In between them is Smothers Park, a two-story playground three city blocks long that has been called one of the ten best playgrounds in the world. It has a splash park for the kids, a VFW War memorial plaza, concession stand, benches and swings overlooking the river, and several fountains that were designed by the same company that built the Bellagio fountains in Las Vegas. Only smaller, of course. But they're pretty cool. They're lit up at night and they go off on a timer every fifteen minutes or so to do their little fountain shows.

Once Smothers Park opened up, the foot traffic downtown really picked up and more restaurants and shops started opening downtown again. The building continues today.

A few years ago, the Visitor's Bureau started putting "Owensboro Walk of Fame" plaques along Second Street. There are quite a few celebrities from Owensboro. You may have heard of a few of them. Florence Henderson, who played the mom on *The Brady Bunch*, went to high school here. NBA stars Kenny Higgs and Rex Chapman grew up in Owensboro. So did Mark Higgs, Kenny Willis, Vince Buck, Justin Miller, and several other NFL players. As for pro baseball players, Brad Wilkerson graduated from Apollo High School, which is the same high school I went to. Also, several NASCAR drivers, like Darrell and Michael Waltrip; David, Jeff, and Mark Green; and Jeremy Mayfield. And, of course, the Hayden brothers: Nicky, Tommy, and Roger Lee Hayden, who are famous motorcycle racers. They have a walk of fame plaque together, which is pretty neat. NBA star Rex Chapman was a standout at Apollo High School and then the University of Kentucky Wildcats before going on to the NBA.

Last year the new Bluegrass Music Hall of Fame and Museum opened its doors. It's just about as cool-looking as the Country Music Hall of Fame in Nashville or the Rock & Roll Hall of Fame in Cleveland. It also has an outdoor stage to add to the downtown live music vibe. Bill Monroe, who they call the grandfather of bluegrass music, grew up about thirty miles south of Owensboro, which is one reason the Hall of Fame is here and why this area of Kentucky is known as the "bluegrass, bourbon, and barbecue" region.

The Green River Distillery in Owensboro was included in the Kentucky Bourbon Trail™ and is now considered the western gateway to the Bourbon Trail. People from all over the world visit the Bourbon Trail every year and get their passport booklet stamped, and that's a pretty big deal for Owensboro. Bourbon is big business in Kentucky.

But if you picture a grid about seven city blocks wide and three city blocks deep coming right off the river, that pretty much covers our downtown. Beyond that, the city extends down what used to be an old buffalo trail.

Owensboro is the fourth largest city in Kentucky, behind Louisville, Lexington, and Bowling Green.

Owensboro has grown substantially over the years, but really, it is just a big small town, and that's what I like about it. We might be the biggest city between Louisville and Evansville, but we still have that small-town feel in a good way. Maybe it's Southern charm. But it's got that everybody-looks-out-for-everybody-else kind of feel. People are nice. We smile and wave to each other here. It's not like the big cities.

OWENSBORO'S COMPASSION . . . IT'S WHERE MY ROOTS ARE

"But the true charm and compassion of Owensboro is apparent, anytime a crisis happens. This town comes together and takes care of each other. That's just the kind of people we are."

~JASON

We saw that in 2000 when a tornado came through. I remember taking one of Dad's company backhoes and helping to clear debris from the streets in the neighborhood by Apollo High School. It was hit really hard. I can't tell you how many people were out there volunteering those next couple days to help people get their homes and yards cleaned up.

Crews from Owensboro almost immediately deploy to natural disasters all over the country. And anytime there's a tragedy here, just like with my accident, this town steps up.

We saw the city come together strong in 2017 when Nicky Hayden died. Nicky was the 2006 MotoGP World Champion motorcycle racer. He and his brothers grew up in Owensboro racing all around the country, and around the world, but they all three still lived here. That's what's cool about Nicky. He was still an Owensboro boy. There are other celebrities from Owensboro, but they have moved on. They still come and visit but don't live here. Nicky still had a house here and you'd see him around town and he was just the coolest guy, even though he was a world-famous athlete. This whole community mourned his loss. You still see Nicky Hayden stickers on about half the cars you pass on the street.

I think Nicky liked the small-town feel in Owensboro too. He'd get mobbed in Europe or Japan or other countries where MotoGP racing is as popular to them as football or basketball is in America. But he could just be a guy from Owensboro here, and people would leave him be.

After Nicky died, his family and the City of Owensboro put up a bronze statue downtown in front of the Convention Center. It's modeled after a famous picture of Nicky carrying the American flag around the track on the victory lap after he won the World Championship. A lot of people come to Owensboro just to see that statue because he has fans from all over the world. Nicky, Tommy, and Roger share one of those Walk of Fame plaques I mentioned earlier. They were one of the first installed.

Nicky Hayden was a superstar and always represented the best of everything that's good about Owensboro. His family still does.

The month after my accident, there was a big fundraiser to help with hospital expenses and all three Hayden brothers donated stuff to auction off. We aren't best buds or anything, but we are acquaintances for sure, and I'll never forget them going the extra mile like that to help with that fundraiser.

Now Nicky's legacy carries on off the track. There were so many tributes to Nicky and fundraisers for the memorial fund that his family started in his honor to give grants to children's charities in Owensboro each year. The Hayden family contributed to homeless shelters and children's shelters in his name, too. It's been really cool to see.

I could go on but I think I've given you a sense of what kind of community this is. Owensboro is a special place and these people are amazing.

The truth is, I wasn't made for city life. I like to be where you can hear the crickets and see the stars. Jenny and I live just far enough out of town that we can still see the city lights glow on the horizon from our front porch. But we are still close enough that we can be in town in five minutes.

I don't know if you'd ever find it on any map, but this little area out here is a tiny farm community known as "Browns Valley." Our house sits about a half mile off Highway 431.

This is the land my grandfather owned. After he passed, the farm passed down to the next generation and my uncles and cousins still farm it now. My cousin now lives two houses down, which is where my grandfather used to live. Most of our other neighbors have lived on our county road for generations.

This is the house my parents built and raised me and Holly

in, and it's always been my dream to raise my family here. Thankfully, Jenny liked that idea and my parents agreed to it.

So here we are.

It's a nice piece of property where we can ride four-wheelers out in the fields, enjoy the country air, and watch the clouds go by. Jenny and I put in a pool for the kids. I've got a really nice detached garage where I can tinker on projects. The kids have room to roam.

We love it here.

CHAPTER 3

JENNY

*"There's no way I could have gotten through my accident
or do what I do today without Jenny's support."*
~JASON

Whenever I tell my story, Jenny is always a big part of it. There's no way I could have gotten through my recovery after my accident or do what I do today without her support. She's an amazing woman, an excellent wife, and a great mother. Anybody who knows me can tell you that too.

Our story together really goes back to college though.

The funny thing about Jenny and I is even though we're both from Owensboro, we didn't meet until college two hours away. I went to Apollo High School and Jenny went to Daviess County High School across town. So even though she grew up about five miles from where I did, we never met until we were at Murray State University together.

I actually met her through my friend Jason Strode, who went to church with Jenny. I knew Strode from high school, but he and I were roommates at Murray State. I was still racing cars then, so every Friday afternoon I was coming back home to load up and go racing. It was funny because there were several times when Jenny and some of their other church friends would come down to Murray to hang out with Jason Strode, but we never saw each other then. That was because most weekends I was on my way back to Owensboro at the same time she was heading down to Murray.

Strode would tell stories to Jenny and her friends about his wild and crazy roommate (that would be me) who drove race cars, and here's Jenny who is mild, and timid, and a little shy even. We were like opposites in some ways.

That was my freshman year of college and Jenny's senior year of high school. But my sophomore year at Murray I moved into a fraternity house and Strode moved into his fraternity house, so we weren't roommates anymore, but we still hung out. By then, Jenny was also at Murray.

Strode told me about Jenny and showed me pictures of her. She was definitely pretty and I wanted to meet her. Finally, Strode introduced us at a party one night and we got to talking and sort of clicked and became friends right off the bat. I think if you would ask her, she probably never even considered dating me at first because we were so different. I was the life of the party. Jenny was more laid back.

Every now and then she'd ride home with me instead of us both driving back to Owensboro. At the time, I was dating somebody else and she was too, so we were just friends. Eventually we were both single and started riding back together more and hanging out in Owensboro on the weekends.

That's how it was my junior year, which was her sophomore year. Jenny recalls:

"I would hear Jason Strode talk about his other friend named Jason, but we never met until we were both at college at Murray State. My friend Kim and I were roommates at Murray and we went to an AGR party, which is Alpha Gamma Rho, the fraternity a lot of the agriculture guys were in. That's when I met Jason Koger. I definitely remember that night. I had a boyfriend at the time, and Jason had a girlfriend at Murray, so we were just friends hanging out after that.

"I only stayed at Murray one year. I ended up moving back home to Owensboro and transferred to Brescia University my junior year and my dad died two years later. I feel like that was God's hand in bringing me home so I had more time to spend with my dad.

"Jason and I were just good friends for a while. We spent a lot of time together. He would drive me home while I was still at Murray when I wanted to come home for the weekend or whatever.

"Murray State's mascot is a 'Racer,' so I was a Racer Girl on the dance team for Murray State. I had a night class and whenever I had to be at the game Jason would come to the middle of campus and pick me up and drive me to my games and things like that. That was all while we were friends."

Since Jenny transferred to Brescia University and moved back to Owensboro, we weren't at school together my senior year. But we'd still hang out on the weekends when I came home.

Finally, I asked her if she wanted to start dating, but we were at this place downtown and the music was pretty loud so she must not have heard me because she completely ignored me. I mean she didn't say *anything*!

But I didn't give up. That's not my nature. I asked her out again a little while later, but she said she wasn't sure because we were such good friends. I asked her out a couple more times, got rejected a couple more times, and finally wore her down from pestering her enough because she finally said yes.

We've been together ever since.

My parents would tell you they thought Jenny was the one for me from the first time they met her. My sister, Holly, used to give me a hard time saying things like, "Yeah. Sure she's 'just a friend.'

Yeah, right!" I guess she thought there was something more to me and Jenny before I did.

It wasn't long before I met Jenny's parents too and we got along really well. I'll let Jenny say more about her dad, Billy, in a minute, because that's her story to tell, but I do sometimes wonder what it would be like if Jenny's dad was still around. Especially after my accident. Billy could rig up anything. I have no doubt that he would have been a huge help to us after my accident, just like Jenny's mom and my parents were and continue to be.

Billy was a mechanic. He was the kind of guy that could wire something to work, or make a little contraption, or figure something out to fix anything around the house. He was very creative and mechanically inclined and I guarantee he could have and would have rigged up some sort of home-made prosthetic device for me from day one, long before I got my real prosthesis.

He would have had so much fun with our kids growing up. He would have come up with fun stuff for our kids to do all the time. I miss Billy a lot.

We named Billie Grace after him, by the way. A lot of times people will ask about her name, and that's where we got it. Jenny always said she wanted to name our first child after Billy, so when we found out we were having a girl, we stuck with that idea and just spelled it with an "ie."

Here's what Jenny had to say about meeting each other, our college years, and dating:

"Anyone who meets Jason knows he's always got a smile on his face. That's definitely one thing that attracted me to him. There are lots of things; like the way he's so giving. Faith was one thing we always had in common right from the start. Even when we were still just friends, faith has always been an important part of our relationship.

"I didn't ever have to wonder if he would be kind. I didn't have to wonder if he trusted me. When we were dating, I could go hang out with my friends and it didn't bother him. Like yesterday I went shopping all day with my best friend, Tara. Sometimes he goes hunting and does his thing. I do my thing. But it's always been that way with us. Even then, when we were dating.

"I needed somebody that trusted me and that I could trust too. I didn't want to have to worry if I came back when I was out with my friends if he was going to be angry or jealous or whatever.

"Jason's not the jealous type. Our relationship is based on trust and comfort. There's never been jealousy or suspicion.

"We were long-distance dating for a few years there. We started dating when I was 20 and we got married when I was 24. He graduated before me because he's a year older. My senior year at Brescia he had graduated and came back to Owensboro. He was living in a townhouse at the time.

"My dad died that year. Jason had written a letter and wrote everything he would have said if he had the chance to ask for Dad's permission to marry me. I didn't know it then, but Jason slipped that letter in my dad's casket right before they closed it in the funeral home.

"A year later, after I finished college, Jason proposed and showed me a copy of that letter that he left with my dad so I could read it. It was really sweet. That's how Jason proposed to me. His sister helped him write it and typed it for him.

"My dad died when I was 22, which is when Jason wrote the letter. He proposed when I was 23, at Christmas of 2003. It was at his townhouse. After we got engaged, Jason bought a small starter house and I got to pick out colors and help with some of the things like that. It was fun. We got married the next September of 2004.

"We decided when we got married that we wanted to wait

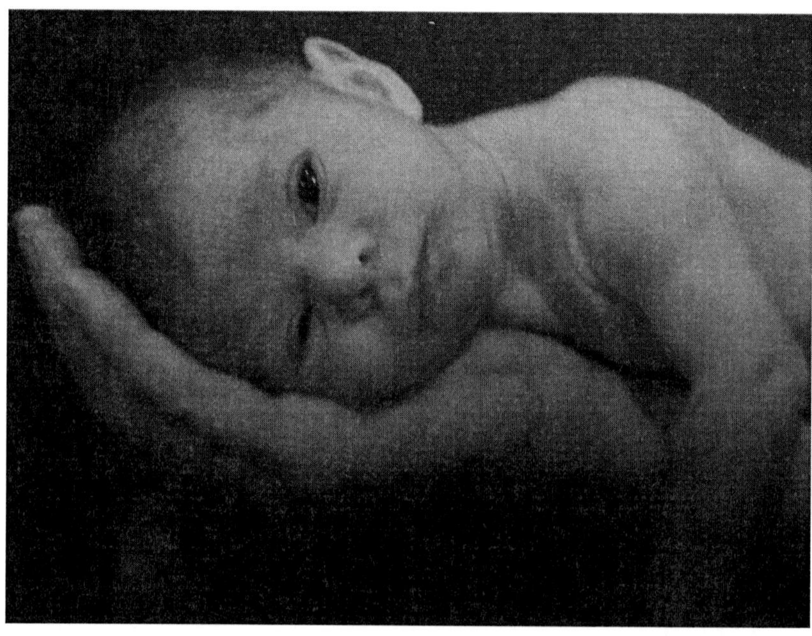

a year to try to have kids. We got pregnant with Billie Grace about a year after we were married. Then Cambell surprised us because the girls were only 18 months apart. No one would ever plan kids that close, right?

"Looking back, even though Cambell was unexpected, it turned out to be another blessing because if she was born later, it would have been right at the same time of the accident. But the way it timed out, Cambell was about 12 weeks old when Jason got hurt.

"Once Cambell came along, it was time to move out of that small house and we decided to move out here to where we live now. Jason basically called his mom and asked if we could buy their house, and they were more than happy to move into town. That had always been Jason's plan.

"We moved out here that August and I had Cambell in December. I had 12 weeks off for maternity leave. I went back for two days and then that Saturday Jason had his accident.

"You have to remember, when Jason was hurt, we hadn't even been married four years yet.

"But the point I want to make here is that our marriage was based on friendship, and our faith, and that our families were already close. As it was, his parents and sister became close to my mom, brother, and sister. We already had those supports in place when the accident happened. We had no way of knowing what was to come, of course.

"At that time, we were still trying to figure things out as a fairly newly married couple raising two young daughters. We were still making changes to the house and getting settled.

"Jason's a wonderful dad. When the kids were little, he would do whatever was needed. He changed a few diapers when I asked him to. But really, he would do whatever was needed. He was happy to help and he was good with the kids. It seemed to come naturally to him.

"Today, he's at every game and every function. It's so important to him. He loves spending time with the kids. He's always been that kind of caring, interactive dad. Even early on.

"We had started a good life together. God had blessed us so much. I think we both always knew God had a purpose for us, as individuals and as a couple. We always knew that.

"It's interesting to look back. We were young, and excited. We both had jobs we loved. Two beautiful girls. Life was happening so fast; we were just hanging on.

"Then the bottom dropped out from under us and we really had to hang on!"

CHAPTER 4

JUST BEFORE THE ACCIDENT

*"After college, I kept on working for my dad's
company and worked my way up to some bigger
jobs. I was really enjoying the work."*
~JASON

Those few years between when we got married to right before my accident went fast. Those were fun times.

By then I had quit racing cars. I raced through high school and college but then I sold it all after Jenny and I got married. It got to be too much. There was too much time away from Jenny, and too much time spent on the car after working all day. I would come home and work on the car until ten or eleven o'clock at night. Then I'd leave on Saturday morning and not get back home until early Sunday morning. After all of that, I'd drag back to work on Monday. It started causing a strain on us. When I began realizing that, I knew it was time to end it. I got out of it before we had kids.

I didn't have much time to miss it, honestly, because I was working on bigger projects for Mom and Dad's business.

I said earlier that I think my parents' example of faith and hard work really paid off for me. Mom and Dad started their business in 1984, when I was still small. I've heard them tell the story several times that they started with $1,500 dollars. Dad would work an eight-hour work day and then do side jobs several hours each night.

There were years Dad might miss Christmas because of an outage at the paper mill or something like that. He worked a lot of hours getting the business going when Holly and I were growing up.

After college, I kept on working for my dad's company and worked my way up to some bigger jobs. I was able to join the Local 633 Plumbers and Pipefitters Union too. I'm proud to be a Union member, and as you'll see later, they've come through for me in a huge way since my accident and continue to support what I do today. I could never thank them enough.

When you get in the union, you go through four years of training. But I sort of got fast- tracked in because of my experience.

After I graduated from Murray State, Dad put me in charge of a job in Hopkinsville at a veterinarian office. It sticks out in my mind because it was a pretty big project, but there were several others. Here's what my dad, Mike, remembers about that project:

"One time I went down there and Jason was sweeping and straightening some broken cinder blocks and things like that. I said, 'What are you doing that for, Jason?' He said, 'Well, I was just cleaning up.' I told him, 'In that guy's contract he is the one to be doing that. Your job is to be the boss and supervise. If things don't look right, then you make him correct it. And this is one thing right here that's not right. Part of his contract is housekeeping.'

"But it was a successful job, the doctor was happy and gave Jason a lot of compliments. Because of that, I knew I could send him on to other jobs, too.

"That was the best way for him to learn. The guys worked well with him, too. So from that time on, he kept moving up to the point that I knew someday he would take our company over and run it and do well with it, if that's what he wanted to do."

At the time of my accident, I was a foreman on a job at a community college. It was a really good job for me to learn how to stay on a timeline and how to run a project. It was fun.

I was putting in a lot of hours the weeks and months before the accident. I was working what we called six, seven, 12s. Twelve-hour days six or seven days a week.

I was really enjoying the work, and they say I was pretty good at it. If I hadn't gotten hurt, I'd probably still be doing that type of work today and would have been content doing that.

But as you'll read in the next chapter, everything changed.

CHAPTER 5

MARCH 1ST, 2008

"I wasn't too concerned about losing my life when it first happened. It just looked and felt like bad burns to me."
~Jason

It still blows my mind that people ask me to come give speeches. My story is unique, but at the same time, it's not that different from anybody else's. We all have struggles. We all have unexpected things happen to us. Tragedies. Trials. Death of somebody we love. Or facing some disease. Everybody has something.

In that sense, I'm no different than anybody else. It's just that you can tell by looking at me what my tragedy was. Most people carry their tragedies around inside and they are not as visible as my wounds.

We all have scars from life. The question is how do we handle them?

Do they define us?

Do we stop living?

Do we give up? Or get back up?

I usually don't get into the details of my accident in my speeches because that's not the time or place. I really can't within a 30-minute talk anyway. Plus, I don't want to get into those details because that's not the point. The point is what's happened in my life since the accident. That's why during a speech I just brush past it quickly and say I was electrocuted and leave it at that so I can get right to the important stuff.

But I'm also aware that people are curious and they really want to know the details of what happened and how I lost my arms.

So what I'm about to explain to you is something people who have seen one of my talks online or in person have never heard before.

To be fair, this is a long chapter, so get comfortable and settle in because this is a wild ride and it moves pretty quickly. The best way I can think to explain what happened is to just take you through the day. Sort of like a play-by-play.

SATURDAY, MARCH 1, 2008

"It's strange to think about because there are so many things I'll never forget about that day. But at the same time there's so much I can't remember."

~JASON

Early morning

I do remember that it was a warm, sunny day. It was the first day of March, and the first really nice day we had that spring. Which is one of the reasons I couldn't wait to get on the four-wheeler and ride around the fields.

Jenny and I had been working on the house, renovating and updating some things. So on that Saturday morning we woke up and I got started on my "honey-do list" because we had talked the night before about some things we wanted to get done that weekend.

Early that morning, before my accident, I was working on

hanging a ceiling fan and I had all the parts and tools that I would need laid out and ready to go.

9:00 a.m.

I didn't get much farther because we took the girls to the mall to let them ride the train. That spring they had this little train that kids could ride around the inside of the mall. We met Holly and Toby and their kids there, too. We did that and came back home because Jenny had a few other projects she wanted me to get done that afternoon.

I had already taken the ceiling fan in the kitchen down before we left, so when we got back home, I was working on putting the new ceiling fan back up. But I stopped and set that aside because some of Jenny's family came over. We had just put the girls down for a nap. I went outside and was playing with the boys who were visiting. They wanted to play basketball, so we shot a couple baskets. Which, now that I think about it, means that other than riding my four-wheeler, shooting a basketball was the last thing I did with my arms intact.

1:00 p.m.

With it being such a nice warm day, I decided to take a quick four-wheeler ride around the farm, so I went back in and told Jenny I'd be right back.

That was nothing out of the ordinary. I had taken that same little loop around the field hundreds of times before. It was early afternoon as I pulled the four-wheeler out of the shop and puttered down the lane. Just a nice slow ride to enjoy the day, feel the sunshine, see the property, and check on things.

The air was crisp, with only a few lazy clouds in the sky. The way our property sits, our house is right off the road. My grandparents left plots of land to each of their kids. Jenny and I live in what was my mom and dad's house, which is the first in a line of five houses of family members. My uncle Larry lives right next door to us and my cousin Charlie lives in the next house, which is my granddad's homeplace. My uncle Mike lives on the other side of Charlie. So when I say our family's property, I'm talking about the fields that sprawl out behind our houses. This is good, Kentucky farmland, which means it's mostly flat but there are gentle slopes with ditch lines separating the fields. You can see for miles back there. It's so peaceful.

My little shop sits behind our house in the side yard, along a gravel lane that goes back to a red barn that sits just uphill from our house. That red barn overlooks the fields that my uncles and cousins still farm.

My usual loop is down that gravel lane past the barn, then a left at the edge of Granddad's field, then along the little path between our field and a larger field adjacent to us. Then there's another left that takes you back to the grain bins at Charlie's house. It's a big square, maybe a quarter of a mile, and it usually takes me about five minutes.

Just before that second left to head back toward the house, there's a little culvert where a small ditch runs down through the larger fields. Along that ditch, there's a utility pole that guides a power line toward a pump house out in the center of the fields. That power line powers a pump that drains the fields if the backwater gets too high.

That power line is a three-eighths-inch line that runs overhead from our red barn, over to the ditch line pole to pole. Then it follows the ditch line overhead pole to pole out to the little pump house out in the middle of the big fields. Well, I didn't know it at the time, but one of the guidewires had broken off one of the poles, which made the pole lean in one direction, which caused the power line to sag in between the leaning pole (to my left) and the next pole (to my right). Unbeknownst to me, that sagging line was a few feet off the ground directly ahead of me on my route. We bushhog (which means to clear the heavy brush) that path I was on so four-wheelers or tractors or whatever can get back to the fields.

They rotate crops, so one year they plant corn and another year they plant soybeans. The year before, the field directly ahead of my path had been planted with corn, so the cornstalk clippings were still brown from the winter and they hadn't been tilled up yet. Because it was early in the spring, the green sprouts hadn't quite broken through the ground yet. The sky was blue, and the afternoon sun was bright, but the land was still covered in shades of brown. I was looking far beyond my path at the quiet setting.

I had no way of knowing that a power line had dropped low enough for me to come in contact with it, and with it only being three-eighths of an inch, it's hard to see in the first place.

Plus, from my vantage point at that particular spot just before I got to that culvert, the lay of the land slopes upward a little bit across the other side of the culvert, making that little wire blend in with the cut-down cornrows on the opposite hill. The line was nearly invisible because it was camouflaged into the background with the cornrows that were running the same direction as that tiny black line in my sight line.

I wasn't looking directly in front of me because I was looking out through the fields. I watched a hawk fly way up high in the sky and was enjoying the peaceful scenery around me.

All that to say, I didn't see the downed line.

Not until I felt something thump against my chest. I immediately came to a stop to try to figure out what hit me and realized my four-wheeler had run up under the line. By then it had bounced off my chest and was lying right on the gas tank as I was still sitting on the four-wheeler. Maybe 30 inches off the ground.

As soon as I saw the downed power line lying across both arms, I could feel the adrenaline rush! My heart was pounding! My mind was racing! But my brain couldn't make any sense of what my eyes were seeing. I didn't know what to do or how to react.

I've always been told that if you're on rubber tires like I was, electricity is not going to shock you anyway. That was the first thought I remember having. I figured since that line runs to the pump house, and since it didn't do anything to me, the power must have been shut off so it wasn't live.

But what do I do now?

Should I just raise it up with one hand and drive under it?

Should I back away slowly and carefully?

Or slam it in reverse and get out of there as quickly as possible?

I was still trying to process it all when I noticed my cousin was out in his yard, which is up on top of the next hill. Maybe he could help me prop it up or something so no one else would hit it. I slowly raised the line up with one hand, carefully drove under it, and once I was clear of it, rode up to my cousin's house to talk it over with him. I didn't want anybody else to get hurt, or some other kid on a four-wheeler to run up on it and get decapitated or something awful like that.

My cousin and I talked about it and I told him we needed to do something to prop that line up out of the way. At that point, I had no thoughts anymore about electricity or being electrocuted since I had assumed the power was shut off.

By then my heart rate had slowed back down and I was shaking it off, thinking I was no longer in any danger. I was thankful and relieved nothing bad had happened, but also concerned about somebody else getting hurt.

My cousin jumped on his four-wheeler and followed me back down there to see if we could fix it somehow. My idea was maybe we could prop a two-by-four underneath the line and hold it up so nobody else would run into it until the electric company could come out and fix the guidewire and straighten the pole back up to get the wire back in place. But that might take a few days until they could come.

When we got back down there, my cousin and I were both on our four-wheelers talking it over. I was right by the wires. He was right behind me. Just a few feet away.

This is where it gets a little foggy in my memory. I remember saying something like, "All we'd have to do is have it this high." The way I remember it, I was pointing to the line but not actually touching it. I'm not 100% clear if I was closer than I thought and accidentally touched it, or if the electricity jumped somehow or what, but *that's* the exact moment I got electrocuted.

Not the first time, when the wire definitely touched me and I clearly remember hitting it. But the second time, when I assumed it was shut off and I may or may not have even touched it.

Nobody really knows why.

I've heard stories that it could have been caused by a blade of grass that brushed against me. Or the current could have jumped off the line over to me and shocked me. But for whatever reason, it made a circuit, it became hot, and I got shocked. Something had to make a ground though. Maybe I hit the bottom line and the top line at the same time without realizing it and that's why it shocked me. Who knows?

But it's just one more mysterious thing about the whole

situation. Why did it not shock me the first time? Why did it shock me the second time when I came back down there with my cousin? I have no idea.

I don't remember the jolt. The last thing I remember was pointing at the line, but I must have blacked out from the surge of electricity because the next thing I remember was waking up on the ground, on my back, facing the opposite direction, so it was obviously enough to throw me off my four-wheeler.

I've been told it was 7,200 volts. Definitely enough to kill somebody. In fact, I've also been told that an electric chair is 6,900 volts. But it didn't kill me for some reason. I don't remember seeing anything, but the way my cousin described it to me later made me picture fireworks on the Fourth of July.

From what others tell me, it most likely shocked me for 30 seconds before the breaker tripped off. And based on what doctors told me later, what most likely happened is my whole body tensed up and my hands must have clenched the line with enough force to rip all the tendons in both hands, based on what they found during the surgery later that night because they said my tendons had snapped like rubber bands and wrapped around my wrist bones.

Someone told me it could have been that my heart stopped. And maybe it started back when I hit the ground. I don't know why it didn't kill me when it obviously should have, but my life was spared.

Most people assume the electricity blew my arms off. That's not what happened. The amputation that night to save my life is what took my arms, not the initial shock.

But it did do some serious damage. My left thumb was blown almost completely off. Seeing my thumb dangling awkwardly was enough to freak me out a little bit, but other than that, I wasn't too concerned about losing my life when it first happened. It just felt and looked like bad burns to me.

There's no way to know which wounds were entrances or exits, but there was a hole about the size of a pencil eraser on my hand between my ring finger and middle finger and a couple burn holes in my chest. The electricity also blew a hole out the side of my foot that was shaped like a check mark. If you look at the brake on the side of a four-wheeler, it's shaped like a check mark. It also blew my tennis shoe off. The EMTs on the scene said my shoe was about 30 feet away.

As I was regaining my senses, I remember noticing the four-wheeler was still running, even though I was lying on the ground next to it.

That's when I realized my hands felt like they were on fire!

My cousin called 911 and then called his dad, my Uncle Mike, who was there right away. He said when he got there, I was trying to crawl into the ditch to put my hands in the muddy water to cool them off. A doctor told me later when you're electrocuted your body feels like it's 115 degrees. That makes sense because I was burning on the inside. My arms were red like a really bad sunburn with white blisters from the third-degree electrical burns, but I felt hot all over, outside and inside. It was the strangest feeling.

The only way I can describe it is that it felt similar to holding your hand close enough to a flame that you can feel the heat and your brain tells you to pull your hand away. Except there was no way to pull my hand away. It was that constant sensation of intense heat, and it was in both of my arms.

My cousin Charlie came pretty quick. He waited at the road and flagged the ambulance down to point them to where I was back in the field. They said there was a lot of confusion about how bad things were and nobody wanted to be the one to tell

Jenny because they didn't know what to say. Charlie called my mom. Holly was right there so she took the phone from my mom and called Jenny.

Here's what my mom remembers about that phone call:

"When Charlie called, my immediate thought was maybe it was one of my brothers who had been hurt in a farm truck or something. When he said Jason had been hurt, I could tell by his voice that it must be really bad. So I asked if he was alive. And Charlie just kind of stumbled and didn't know what to say. So that's why I started screaming.

"He told me Jason was on the four-wheeler and they're working on him. I don't remember after that, but Holly took the phone from me."

While that was going on, Jenny was still at the computer working on invitations. I've heard her tell her side of the story several times over the years, and the way she describes it, she didn't think much about the power going out because that happens every now and then. She didn't know there was a problem until Holly called her.

Here's the way she remembers it:

"I didn't know all that was going on out in the field. All I knew was Holly called me and was frantic on the phone and was saying that Jason had been in an accident.

"I'm thinking, did he flip his four-wheeler? Did he get hit on the road? Or what? What did she mean?"

From what the neighbors told us later, it shut down the power to the whole neighborhood. One lady said she could see exactly what time it happened because it was on the clock on her stove where it reset after the power went out.

The details of those first minutes back there in the field are fuzzy to me now. I know my cousin and my uncle were right there with me. The next thing I remember was the ambulance coming to get me, which obviously was a little bit later, so I must have been in and out of consciousness.

The first person I remember talking to, besides my cousin Travis, was Kevin, a family friend who's also a first responder and got the call that day and came right away.

My neighbor across the street came down. My other neighbor saw a truck tearing down through the field and came out to see what was wrong.

My cousin Charlie, the one who called my mom, waited at the end of the road for the ambulance.

Our neighbor Mark is the one who drove Jenny back to the field. Jenny made it to me about the same time the ambulance got there. Here's how she described the ride back to the field:

"After I got off the phone with Holly, I left my brother's fiancé with the kids and ran outside to check on Jason. I ran out of the garage and didn't see anything. I looked at the shop and the lane and didn't see anything.

"But I did see our neighbor across the street had run across the yard yelling, 'What's wrong? What happened?' I yelled, 'I don't know, but something has happened to Jason!'

"Mark grabbed the keys to Jason's truck and drove me back into the field. That's when we could see the lights of an ambulance flashing. I must have heard the sirens but in all the commotion it was like I couldn't process it all. They must have gotten there right before we did.

"I remember Holly told me later on that nobody wanted to call me. I think they were seriously afraid it was going to be really bad and they didn't know what to say.

"I don't know how much time had passed but there was enough time for the ambulance to get there and start working on him because when I got there, they already had Jason on a stretcher and he was talking."

I remember Jenny being fairly calm, but very concerned of course. When she first saw the four-wheeler she couldn't figure out how or why I got hurt. She didn't know if I flipped it or what happened. I tried to stay calm and told Jenny, "It's really not that big of a deal. I just might lose a thumb."

I could tell everyone around me thought it was bad, but I had no idea yet how bad it really was.

All I knew is I was hurting like crazy, and I was confused. That hot feeling was like nothing I had ever experienced before. It was intense! I don't remember being panicked or in the fear of death like it was a life-threatening thing, though. That thought hadn't entered my mind yet. It never really did, actually. I could see the fear and concern in other people's faces, especially the EMTs when they got there. I could tell they were taking this very seriously.

They loaded me into the ambulance and Jenny jumped up front with the driver. She says I was still completely coherent at that point, but I kept repeating myself and telling her I was going to be okay and everything was going to be fine. As the ambulance raced to the local hospital, Jenny called our parents to let them know we were on the way.

Jenny remembers:

"Right as we were pulling into the hospital the driver told me they would probably have to take him to another trauma unit somewhere else for his electrical burns. At that point, I still hadn't realized he had been electrocuted. I still thought he had just been in a four-wheeler accident and hurt his hand and his arms. I didn't make the connection between the power going out and him getting hurt at the same time.

"When the driver told me something about electrical burns it was still confusing to me. Then when we went into the emergency room, I could see that everyone in there was really high-pressure. The staff was moving around very fast, almost frantic. I remember the doctor saying, 'This kid's going to lose his hands if we don't get him out of here.' Which was also confusing to me because at that point I just couldn't understand how that would even be an option.

"Then the rest of the family started showing up."

When my parents got to the emergency room, they could tell everyone was in panic mode. The image that sticks out in my dad's mind from that moment was seeing me with my arms bandaged up with a little spot of blood where my thumb used to be. He didn't know at that time that I had lost it.

He says he'll never forget my first words to him as they wheeled me by him were, "Dad, I wasn't going fast." (On the four-wheeler.)

He looked down at me and said, "Jason, I wasn't worried about you going fast, we're just going to get you better."

Doctor Knight at Owensboro Health Regional Hospital explained to Jenny and my parents that they were going to fly me to the trauma center at Vanderbilt in Nashville.

That left our families scrambling to figure out what to do with all our kids so they could get to Nashville as fast as possible. Toby's parents came and got their kids. Jenny's mom and aunt Kaye came and stayed at our house with Billie Grace and Cambell. Luckily, Jenny's mom had been around enough that she already knew their routines. My parents drove as fast as they could to Vanderbilt, which is normally a two-hour drive. Jenny stayed back to sign paperwork so they could fly me by helicopter. She wanted her sister right by her side. Toby also stayed back so he could drive Jenny and her sister to Nashville.

Toby put the pedal to the metal and drove Jenny and her sister as fast as he safely could to meet me at Vanderbilt. Toby recalls:

"We were all emotional, of course. It was an intense drive. Jenny's sister being with her was powerful to see. I remember Jenny and her sister talking through scenarios. Wondering about the kids. Trying not to think too far about what this means for the future. At some point it turned to a conversation of faith and putting trust in the Lord that He would have the best outcome from the situation.

"A lot of that drive is a blur in my mind, but I do remember being amazed by Jenny's strength. She was thinking level-headed and putting her faith first. Jenny's sister did a great job of calming her down and keeping her even-keeled and talking big-picture and focusing on faith. She was assuring her everything was going to be okay. and reminding her the Lord's got this. There would be a new normal but everyone would deal with it. There was quite a bit of prayer. There were some prayers said out loud and in silence to ourselves, too.

"As my sister-in-law, I knew Jenny pretty well, but you don't really know someone until you're put in a situation like that. It was eye-opening for me to see that level of faith."

VANDERBILT – SATURDAY EVENING

"Nurses were moving me very quickly from one room to the next and I'd get little glimpses of people in the hallways. It still felt surreal, like I was watching a really intense movie scene, except I was in it!"

~JASON

They loaded me into the helicopter feet first. I was so crammed in there it felt like my feet were almost touching the front windshield. It was cramped, it was loud, and it was shaky, but I tried to stay calm.

There was an attendant whose job must have been to watch over me the whole time. She was stationed right at the head of my gurney, looking straight down at me. There was another attendant at my side, and between the two of them, they were constantly checking on me, asking questions, keeping me talking. It was nonstop movement, with beeps and noises and the muffled rumbling of the propellers outside. I could also hear radio chatter between the pilot and the people waiting for us down at Vanderbilt.

It turns out the flight path from Owensboro to Nashville flies directly over my granddad's farm so I turned my head to the side and could see there were still emergency vehicles and sirens flashing in the field.

The other thing I remember about the helicopter ride is kind of gross, but they had me hooked up to a catheter and my urine was really dark, almost like maple syrup. They said it was because electrical burns cause poisonous toxins inside your body and my kidneys were filtering all those toxins as best they could, but it was just too many. I later found out there was a serious chance my kidneys could have completely shut down from working too hard.

While all that was going on, Dr. Jeffrey Guy, the surgeon at Vanderbilt who performed the surgeries that saved my life, had been paged and was mentally preparing for surgery. I found out later that he had been on the phone with the ER in Owensboro to help them do what they could and was getting the team ready for my arrival at Vanderbilt.

I think it's fascinating to hear Dr. Guy's perspective. Especially what was going on in his mind in preparation for the surgeries and things I never knew at the time. (You will read more about that later.) He and the whole staff at Vanderbilt took such good care of me and I'll be forever grateful.

It's really spotty in my memory as I look back on it now. I'm sure I was in shock. And I might have been in and out, but there's still so much I remember too.

The flight didn't feel long, but I was glad to get out of that cramped helicopter. As soon as they opened the helicopter doors it was full speed ahead. Everyone was in high gear, wheeling me from the helipad into the hospital and rushing me into the elevator to the burn unit floor. I caught a quick glimpse of the Nashville sky as they wheeled me inside, but that little bit of peacefulness turned into more hospital noises and voices as soon as they wheeled me into the elevator. I remember lying there looking straight up and the ceiling of the elevator as it began lowering me down. Then, when those doors opened, it was just like those hospital shows on TV where all the patient sees is faces looking down on them as the hallway lights blur past.

Except this wasn't TV. It wasn't a dream. This was real!

Then, as soon as they wheeled me into the hallway of the burn unit, I saw some faces I actually knew. Jenny had an aunt and uncle who happened to be in Nashville that day, so they came to Vanderbilt and made it there right before I did. My cousin Hadley was waiting there too. I was surprised to see her but found out later my dad called and told her to come so I'd see a familiar face. She leaned over, kissed me on the forehead, and I remember her saying, "It's going to be okay."

I had been telling myself that, but it was so nice to hear that from a familiar face. I'll never forget that.

Next, they took me down the hallway and into a room that was very bright like an operating room, but everything was stainless steel and very sterile looking. Like what a morgue looks like on TV shows. And it was chilly in there. I was still feeling like my whole body was burning hot, so that cold room took my breath away for a minute. I found out later that was the hydro room in the burn unit where they basically pressure-wash the dead skin off third-degree burns.

At that point, they hadn't given me any pain medicine because Jenny wasn't there yet to sign the papers for treatment. They were also afraid to give me any more medicine for fear my kidneys would shut down because they were fighting so many toxins already.

Dr. Guy explained:

"We start in hydro to do a good assessment. People get so caught up and paralyzed by the obvious injuries. But what we don't want to do is overlook any unseen life-threatening injuries. With burns, it's really easy to do. You have these horrific obvious injuries but what you don't see is a possible intracranial bleed. Or a ruptured spleen where the patient could be bleeding in his abdomen or something like that.

"That's why we do CT scans in hydro for brain and abdomen to rule out any major concern there. Then we knew we could deal with his arms and he's not going to bleed to death in the operating room because of a liver laceration or never wake up again because of an unseen brain bleed.

"There aren't many injuries that scare me. Gunshot wounds and car crashes and things like that don't scare me because for the most part a bullet causes a hole and you patch the hole and stop the damage. But electrical injuries always scare me because you don't know what you're dealing with beneath the surface.

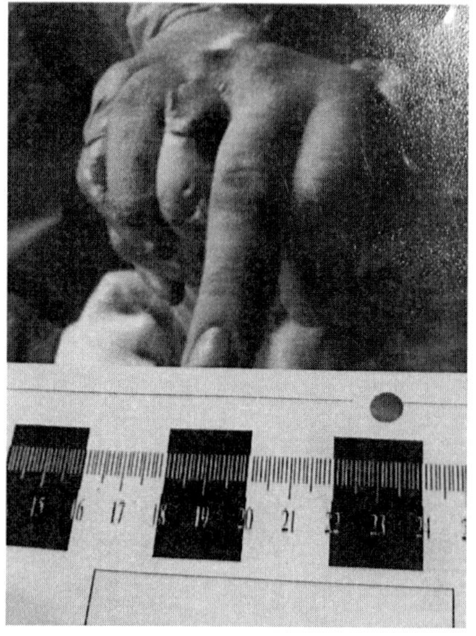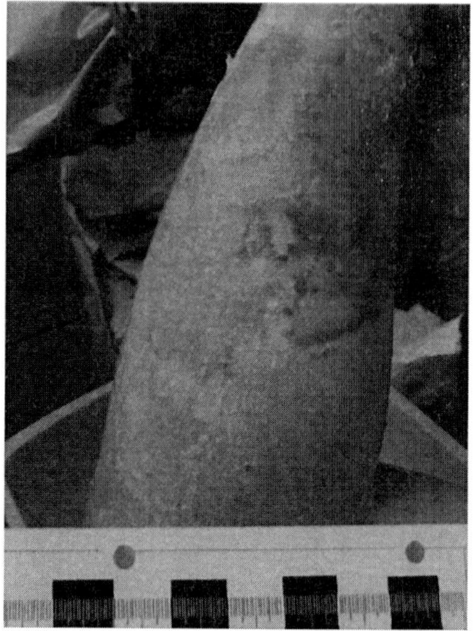

ERs will call you and say there's a small contact wound here and a small contact wound there but what's in your mind is that the patient is burned from the inside out, because that's what happens with these electrical injuries. Electrical injuries are bad.

"I could fill a room with former patients with high-tension electrical injuries like Jason's. I've had several where we've had to amputate all the way up at the shoulders.

"With Jason's injury in particular, like most, we don't try to label the wounds 'entrance' and 'exit' wounds because it's very hard to tell where the electricity went in and out of the body. We refer to them as 'contact points.'

"It was high-tension so it was direct current. Jason says it was 7,200 volts. It had to go in somewhere and come out somewhere. But we just never know exactly where it came in, where it went inside the body, and where it left the body.

"Sometimes we do see jump marks where the electricity jumps across the joint. For example, at the elbow. Jason had several contact points on his arms and chest, left thumb, and a small one

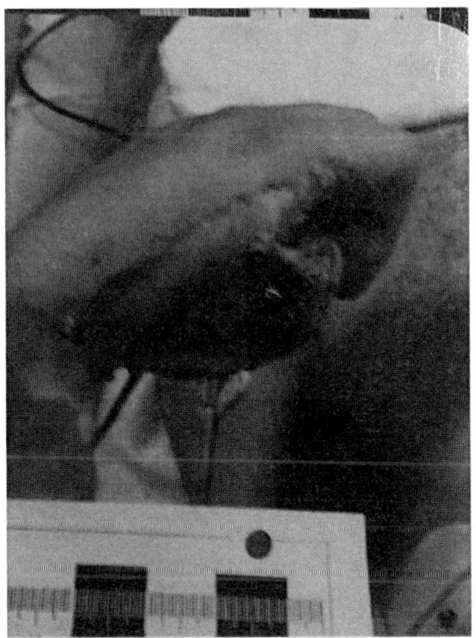 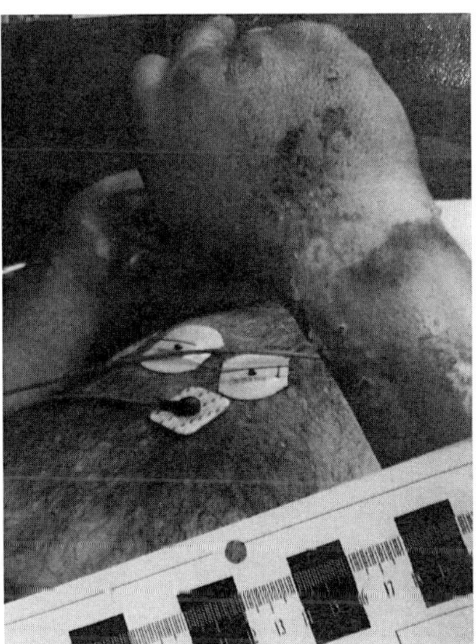

on his foot. So likely the electricity went up his arms and jumped to his thorax. That's where we get nervous because the heart is in the middle of the chest of course."

As soon as hydro was over, Dr. Guy had Jenny sign a release form to give permission for whatever was needed to save my life.

I was able to see Jenny for just a few seconds, and I was so happy she was there with me. They had a lot of work to do on me, and they were very quick about it, so we didn't have much time together except to say things would be okay. She leaned down and kissed me and I told her not to worry.

But I was scared. I didn't know what to expect and I just wanted the pain to stop.

The last thing I remember is being wheeled into the operating room. I don't remember anything else until I woke up from sedation three days later.

With Jenny's face still in my mind as I closed my eyes, all I could do was trust God, trust the doctors, and keep on praying in my mind until I drifted off to sleep for three days.

CHAPTER 6

SURGERY

*"Jason touches people because of his resilience . . . I think
most people can see a little of themselves in his story
because we all face challenges. It's an amazing story."*
~Dr. Jeffrey Guy

I was about to take a big nap for three days while Dr. Guy and his team did what they had to do to save my life. Everything in this entire chapter was told to me later on by Jenny, Dr. Guy, and my mom and dad.

I've heard bits and pieces of those three days retold over the

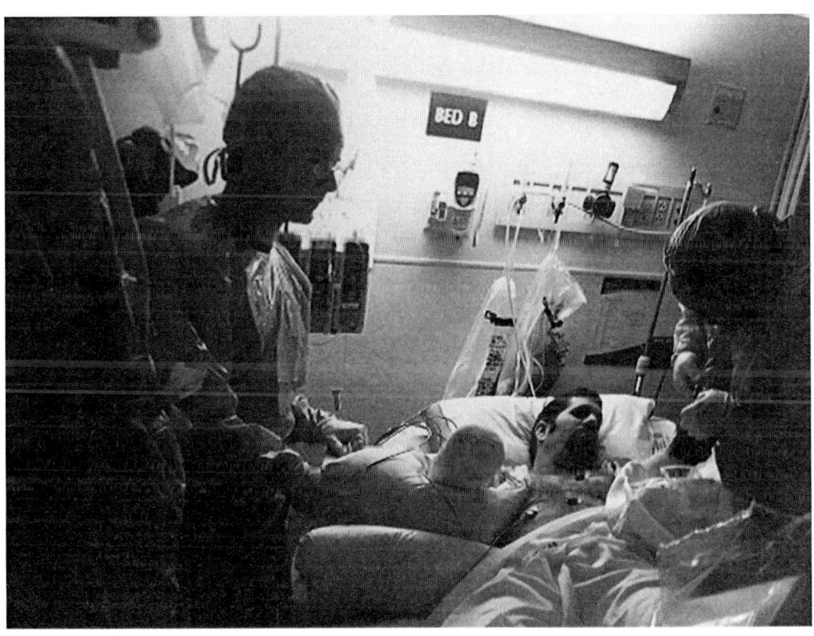

years but working on this book gave me a chance to revisit this part of my story with those who were there.

This section is what they remember about those three days while I was sedated. What you'll be reading next will be told from Jenny's perspective.

THE FIRST SURGERY – SATURDAY NIGHT

"In that first surgery, we took tissue back to the point we knew that tissue was still alive. But what you don't know is if that same tissue is going to still be alive the next day."
~Dr. Jeffrey Guy

[As told by Jenny Koger]

I was able to see Jason for just a few seconds before they took him to surgery. They were moving quickly. I remember seeing Jason lying on the gurney. He had an oxygen mask on, and I saw a single tear run down his face. He kept telling me it would be okay, but seeing that tear told me he was as scared as I was. I'll never forget that.

Then they got to work on Jason and they took us into a family room. I had to sign more papers to give them permission for a blood transfusion or whatever they needed to do. I know they used the word "amputation," but at that moment, I still didn't think it would ever come to that. It just didn't seem that serious. I remember seeing that bad spot on his thumb. But apparently, it was the other arm that was worse. It still just seemed so surreal then.

Jason's dad, Mike, was there with me, and could see I was feeling a little overwhelmed. He remembers that moment.

"Dr. Guy came into that little waiting room with the papers for Jenny to sign and told us what was going on at that point. He told us the main thing was they were afraid his kidneys were going to fail from all the poison. He did tell us there was a chance they would have to amputate. It was a lot for Jenny to take in. She wilted, about to pass out, like anybody would.

"But I just told her, 'Jenny, you're going to have to sign those papers. I know it's hard. But you have to do it.'"

When we talked about it later, I think both of us at that point were thinking Jason might possibly lose his thumb, not both of his arms.

But I did sign those papers because that's what you have to do. And of course I wanted them to take care of my husband, however they had to.

All I could do was pray and trust.

In Dr. Guy's mind, there was no question about going to surgery that night. He explained to us that with most wounds, when the injury happens the damage is done. But with electrical burns, the damage can continue in the muscles. Here's how Dr. Guy explained the first surgery:

"Our plan was to be as conservative as possible. Usually, you have to go back for additional surgeries every few days. That's why we had Jason sedated for several days so he could be asleep and comfortable so we could go back in to check the tissue and save as much length as possible. The more you're able to save, the better function the patient will have later on and you have a better chance of getting a good fit for prostheses.

"One of the things we don't understand is electricity will travel through water and it heats up the bone. A lot of times what will happen is the muscle will look pretty normal at first, but what we can't see is if the electricity went in or out of the bone, and where it may have traveled. Sometimes the electricity superheats the bone and continues to damage the tissue the next few days. So that's what we didn't know about Jason's condition.

"The other thing is electricity goes through fluid, and your arms are mostly fluid. Blood vessels are smooth like glass. And they could be damaged by the current too. The patient could actually get blood clots developing in blood vessels. What we explained to the family is we took the tissue as far back as it was dead and left as much length as we could for the advantage of the patient. But we always have to go back and keep checking the next few days. We typically anticipate that for the first five to seven days.

"When muscle gets heated like that it can infect your heart. It can cause intracranial bleeds. All this stuff we were worried about. When muscle cooks it releases a toxin called myoglobin that comes out in your kidneys and turns urine a dark brown color. It will kill the kidney. If that happens, you're spending the rest of your life on dialysis. That's why we did the amputation the way we did as fast as we could. We amputated his arms as quickly as we could to get him in and out as quickly as possible. We knew we were going back in. We knew we would revitalize the tissue later. We were trying to give him as much length as possible. In Jason's case, it was trying to save his elbows.

"It was late at night. Maybe 10 o'clock. We did what we had to do in the operating room to save Jason's life."

While that was going on, a big group of friends and family members had gathered with us in the waiting room, but I honestly couldn't even tell you who was there. I know that sounds bad, but it was a blur to me.

Jason's mom, Donna, remembers there being 45 or 50 people

there. One of them was Mike and Donna's good friend, Fr. Tony Jones, because someone from Owensboro flew him down right after Saturday evening mass.

After Dr. Guy was finished with the first surgery, he came out into the waiting room to give us an update. When he came down that hallway to the waiting room and saw all those people waiting with us, he had a surprised look on his face. When we saw him we all went over to him. He sat on a little table and was sort of taken aback. He asked Donna, "Are all these people with you all?" And she told him yes.

He sat there and got emotional. He said, "I have never seen this many people before. This tells me who Jason Koger is."

Dr. Guy has never forgotten that moment either. Here's how he remembers it:

"At Vanderbilt, the surgical waiting room is the lobby. It looks like a big, open bus stop; everyone is just all out there together. At ten o'clock on a Saturday night you'd expect it to be pretty empty. I fully expected to see just a few people when I walked downstairs.

"But when I walked in that whole area was full of people. I'd seen that before only a few times, like if a police officer or fireman gets hurt on the job because half the department shows up. Or maybe for a teenage kid where all the neighborhood and friends and church show up with the family. But for a guy who got flown in on a helicopter from a couple hours away it was just one of the most bizarre things I'd ever seen.

"Jason's wife, mom, and dad were there. Mike, Jason's dad, sort of took on the spokesperson role. He's this big, gregarious guy. He's just one of those guys where you meet him and you just want to hug him.

"But he asked all the right questions. Had all the normal concerns. We told them what we did and why we did it. And that we weren't out of the woods and we'd probably take Jason back to surgery a couple more times over the next few days to check on the tissue."

Mike says the reason Dr. Guy asked if all those people were with us may have partly been to make sure not to give information out to people who didn't need to hear it. But all those people were family, neighbors, and close friends. A lot of them got hotel rooms and stayed the night.

That moment with Dr. Guy in the waiting room was life-altering. I was young: just 27. I'd only been married a few years and had two babies. Plus, my hormones were all out of whack anyway from having a new baby that was only 12 weeks old.

When Dr. Guy came out to talk to me and explained he had to take both arms, I just dropped down to my knees. It hit me so hard. I just fell.

The first thought in my mind was how are we going to take care of these girls?

Jason's such a great dad. Being a good daddy to our girls was such an important role to him. How was he going to do that now?

I was already wondering how I was going to do this for the rest of my life.

It was all so overwhelming. I really never considered that Jason could have not made it through surgery. Or that he actually could have lost both hands, even though I heard it mentioned.

It was the most traumatic moment of my life.

My dad died six years earlier. Then this.

At that moment in my life, I was thinking we are Christians. We tithe. We go to church. We serve. We do all the things we're supposed to do. So, this is going to be okay, right? Of course we're going to be okay. I trust God. But how can something that horrible happen?

I remember thinking my kids are going to grow up, but I'm going to have to take care of Jason forever. I didn't mean that in a mean, ugly way. But at first, in that moment, that's what went through my head.

That's what I felt then.

But you evolve as you grow. Now I can see that God used that whole situation for so much. It not only made Jason a different person. It made me a different person. God used that accident to make us stronger and our marriage stronger. So much good has come from it.

It made me depend on God in a totally different way. It was things like seeing the way God put people in our life to help at the exact moment we needed it. That was true in the very first moments of the accident, there in the hospital, and every day since.

Dr. Guy also explained to us that they had Jason on a ventilator and would keep him sedated for follow-up surgeries. They gave him pain medicine and also medicine that causes amnesia so he wouldn't remember anything those first few days because there were some very unpleasant things.

Dr. Guy would say that was a very bad night for him too. He says it still haunts him because no one goes to medical school to take someone's arms. As a surgeon, he says that's an awful thing to live with

But Jason and I see Dr. Guy as a hero! He saved my husband's life that night. He gave our kids their daddy back. There is no way to ever say "thank you" enough for what he did for our family.

FOLLOW-UP SURGERIES

"Jason touches people because of his resilience. I think most people can see a little bit of themselves in his story because we all face challenges. It's an amazing story."
~Dr. Jeffrey Guy

[Jenny continues]

Those first few days in the hospital are a blur. All those surgery updates sort of run together now. I'm not sure how many follow-up surgeries Jason had those first couple days, but there were several.

It really helped ease my mind that my mom and aunt were staying with the girls at our house. They brought the girls down to Nashville once things were settled so I could see them. My brother flew in from a mission trip, but he was in college and couldn't stay long. My sister, my mom, and my aunt were a huge support to us. Especially with helping to take care of the girls.

My mom had actually come and stayed with us the week before Jason's accident because Jason was working out of town that week, so Mom had already learned Cambell's routine, her sleep schedule, and how to make her bottle. Which was great because when that happened on Saturday, my mom came to our house as soon as she could. She and my aunt stayed with the girls at our house those first few days when we rushed down to Nashville.

When Toby drove me and my sister from the hospital in Owensboro to Nashville, it was such a blessing knowing our girls were taken care of and I could just go without worrying.

We can see clearly how God's hand was over that entire

situation. Looking back on everything that happened the day of the accident, those next few days at Vanderbilt, and every day since, God was right there with the next answer or the next step we needed.

Here's just one of many examples. The next day after the first surgery, when we were all in waiting mode, Donna and Mike were talking and Donna realized they had timeshare points they might be able to use. Donna called Wyndham and explained the situation and why we were in Nashville and asked if there was something close we could use. They gave Donna and Mike a four-bedroom condo to use that week and didn't even cash their points for it. They just gave it to us to help us out. They even came up and brought us a high chair and kept asking what else we needed, anything they could do to help. They didn't charge us a thing.

There was a neighbor whose daughter lived in Nashville and she brought us food. We had other friends down there that would bring us food too.

It was like the next thing we needed, God provided. Whatever we needed, we were truly taken care of.

I immediately started researching everything I could those first few days in the hospital, because I had to do something. I would spend every spare moment I had in the Vanderbilt library reading everything I could online about amputations and prostheses and whatever else I could find. That's how I learned about i-Limbs, which were brand new at the time. From what I was reading, no civilians had them yet. They were mostly used for military vets who were hurt in combat.

That's how I learned that if you could save the elbows, that's always best, which was Dr. Guy's goal from the very first moment. There would be so much more Jason could do if they could keep his elbows. That was all I wanted to hear, that they didn't take his elbows.

So when they gave us the report from his second or third surgery I was so relieved to hear that they were able to still save both Jason's elbows.

Dr. Guy explained to us that the goal of the first surgery was to stop the infection from spreading. But after that, the surgeries were much more calculated and intricate. Thankfully, when they went back in the second and third time to check on the remaining tissue below the elbows, the remaining tissue had not progressively worsened. That was the best news we could have gotten because that meant they were able to leave enough of his lower arms so the prosthetist could make a good fit later on, especially when it comes to myoelectrics.

For three days and nights we basically camped out in the waiting room, or we'd go back and forth to the condo Wyndham let us use.

I think it was the second day in Nashville when my mom and aunt brought the girls to see me for a little bit, so that helped lift my spirits because I was missing them so much. They came back down again a few days later when we were able to take them to see Jason that first time.

I wasn't actually there when Jason woke up. I was back at the condo getting some rest.

Mike was the first person Jason saw. Looking back, that was probably best. They called me as soon as Jason was opening his eyes and I got back as soon as I could.

WAKING UP

"I truly believe that steely stare I saw in that first ten minutes determined the next ten years of his life."
~DR. JEFFREY GUY

As Jason was slowly waking up from the sedation medicine, Donna and Mike walked back to see him through the glass. The doctors and nurses stepped out so Mike and Jason could talk.

It was a very emotional father-and-son moment. Mike says he took a deep breath, looked Jason in the eye, and explained what happened.

"As I walked into the room, Jason was crying a little bit with tears coming down his face. He still had tubes everywhere, but he was trying to say the word 'hands.' I'll never forget that.

"I said, 'Jason. Yes, you've lost your hands. But you're alive and that's the most important thing. I don't know how we're going to make it, but we're going to get through this. We're going to keep moving forward. Your mother and I are out here. Jenny's on her way back. We're with you if you need us.'"

Dr. Guy was standing just outside the room as Mike explained what happened and he could faintly hear Mike's voice through the glass. Dr. Guy told us later,

"I can still picture it today very vividly. It was such a moving moment. I still get choked up thinking about it.

"After Mike walked out, Jason just sat there. His eyes were totally focused on the wall. I remember thinking I wish I knew what was going on in this kid's head.

"I expected him to be thinking about how his life was screwed up. It would be normal for his mind to be full of bad thoughts.

But now, 14 years later and looking back on it, I think he was staring at that wall mentally preparing. Getting his act together. Figuring out how he was going to beat this thing.

"It was quite the look. Staring at the wall. Processing.

"In my mind's eye, that first ten minutes may have determined his next ten years.

"I fully expected to give orders to mildly sedate him again. We had medicine ordered to help him calm down because most people lose it. It would have been totally normal for him to rage out. Scream. Cry. Get angry. Experience all the grief cycle emotions at once. Like anybody would experience from a major loss.

"It was not that.

"It was this steely look.

"That's why I thought for a while that he was internalizing all of it.

"Then we got to know Jason a little more and I realized that was just Jason. But I really thought he was in total denial at first, and at some point, the wheels were going to fall off."

I got back to the hospital shortly after that. Jason was awake and I went in to see him and we spent some time together. He had made it through the surgeries. Now we would begin our new life together.

MY MOTIVATION

"I didn't have time to be depressed because I had a 21-month-old and a three-month-old to take care of."

~JASON

[At this point in the story, Jason is awake. From here the narrative switches back to Jason's perspective.]

My brain was a little foggy when I woke up, but when Jenny walked in, I felt immediately better.

I remember hearing what my dad said, but I don't remember reacting too strongly to it. I was still in and out of it a little bit.

I remember lying there wondering how I'd be able to keep a roof over our heads and how I was going to be able to provide for my family.

But I don't ever remember thinking for a second *I don't want this life.* It was always *How are we going to get through this?* More like survival, not desperation.

Jenny had already been looking at prosthetics and we started thinking things through together. What my new hands might be like. New technology improvements.

Dr. Guy called it my "iron determination." He says they expected me to fall apart at some point those first couple days after I woke up. Years later he told me he was concerned that I was in denial. He sat down and explained to my parents depression might set in once I got home and that sooner or later reality would hit me hard.

I think my determination was because of my kids.

Knowing that I had a wife to support and two young kids to feed meant that giving up was not an option. Especially being raised by a mom and dad like I had where all I ever saw was hard work. Plus such strong community and family support. All of that was important.

But I also say that I didn't have time to go through *Why me, Lord?* I didn't have time to be depressed because I had a 21-month-old and a three-month-old and I did not have time to worry about myself. It was always about getting better for them.

If it weren't for my two girls, I don't know how my story would have ended. I have no clue.

They were my motivation.

CHAPTER 7

RECOVERY BEGINS

*"As far as recovery, there's healing of body
and healing of soul."*
~Dr. Jeffrey Guy

It seems like we eased into things slowly in the few days after I woke up. Dr. Guy told me that recovery was going to be hard. But I kept thinking about my two little girls and I knew I had to recover for them.

One of the things that helped lift me up the most in those early days and even in the days that followed was that my brother-in-law, Toby, set up a CaringBridge account. He'd heard about the free platform from a friend. Their website explains what they do best: https://www.caringbridge.org/. Confronting an illness or injury is one of the most demanding, isolating things you can do. Family and friends are an amazing source of support, but constantly sharing updates with each and every one of them is impractical. CaringBridge replaces countless texts and emails with a free, easy-to-use communications platform.

Toby talks about why he started it and the positive effect that it had on my recovery:

"It was in the early days of texts and Facebook was in its infancy. We were just overwhelmed by people emailing and calling and checking in when Jason had his accident. So, I set up CaringBridge and updated it to let everybody know how he was doing.

"By doing that, we were able to explain the situation and everybody heard the story right from the source. Then we'd put some pictures up from time to time to show his progress. People enjoyed getting updates and sending their well wishes. And Jason definitely enjoyed seeing them. People just flooded that page with encouraging messages for Jason. It kept people up to date but also let people send encouragement to Jason that was very uplifting. A lot of the comments were about his faith and determination and what a warrior he is. He fed on that.

"Someone would read those to him every day to show him how much love and support he had from not only his family and friends but the whole community. Even beyond Owensboro. He has friends from all over so the support and love was very far-reaching."

Every day when I woke up in the morning. the first thing I wanted Jenny or my mom to do was wheel me downstairs to the computer to read the CaringBridge page. It was always encouraging to read because so many friends and family from Owensboro wrote. It must have been hundreds of people.

My family was helping to support me mentally but I also needed to concentrate on healing my body. Dr. Guy explains the typical difficulties:

"If you just look at this like the wounds are healed and we're done, you're probably in the wrong specialty for this kind of surgery. It's one thing to give him a pulse and keep him awake. But we want to give him his life back.

"A young, healthy, active guy with a wife and two small kids; we've got to be thinking about how we get him back to doing the things he enjoys. Otherwise, he will be putting a gun in his mouth. Because that happens.

"That was one of the remarkable things about working with

Jason. We see many cases where the story doesn't end well. But Jason was determined to get his life back.

"My goal was not to just save his life but to give him his life back. I like to give patients a goal. Something they can visualize themselves doing. Your body will do what your mind sees.

"Jason's goal was to hold his girls again."

MY KIDS WERE MY PRIORITY

"I had no idea how I'd be able to take care of myself. The only thing I cared about was holding my kids again."

~JASON

I remember the day Dr. Guy asked me what my number one goal was in my recovery. If there was one thing that I wanted to work toward being able to do, what would it be?

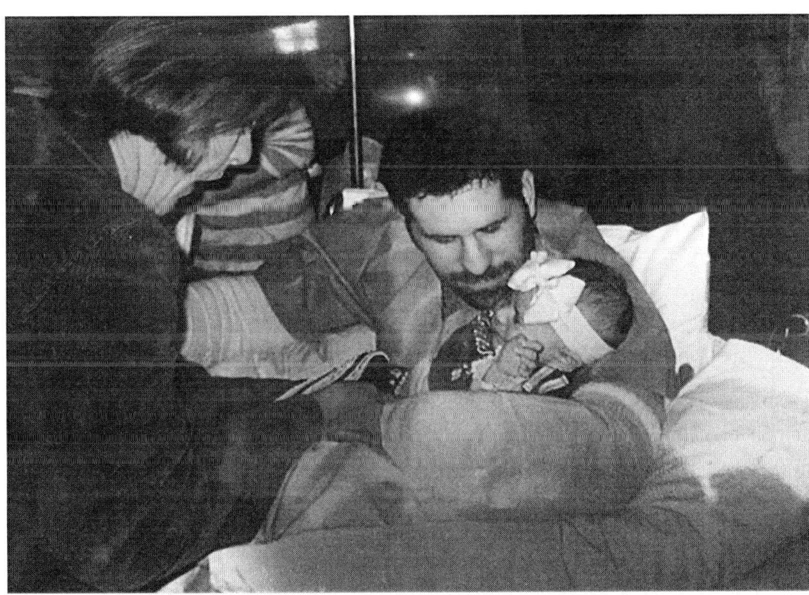

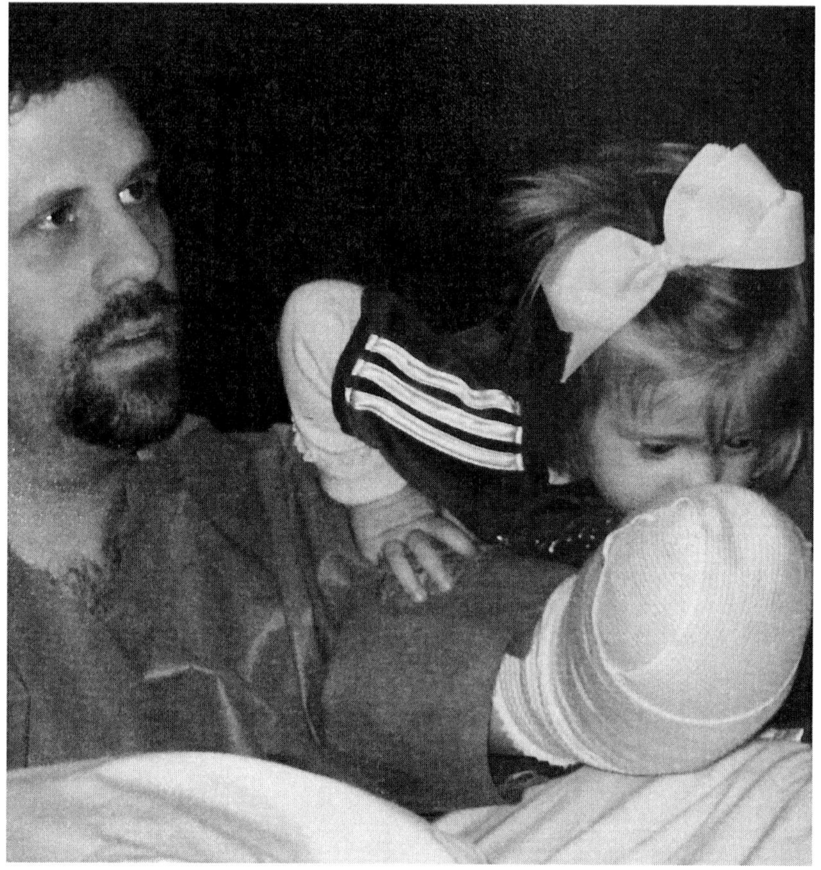

I immediately told him the only thing I care about is holding my kids again. I said I have no idea what my game plan is or how I'll be able to take care of myself. But if I could hold my kids again, that's all I care about. I didn't know if it was possible. But I knew that's what I wanted.

That opportunity came the next day, because Jenny was bringing the girls to the hospital to see me.

Dr. Guy says: "The plan was that the next day we were going to have Jason ready and sitting up in the bed and let Jenny bring the girls in to see him. But Jason didn't want the girls to see him in the room hooked up to all the tubes and machines because he knew they'd be scared already. He wanted them to see him as normal as possible.

"Instead of bringing them into the room, we wheeled him out to the waiting room and the girls saw him for the first time in the lobby and visited with him there.

"I'll always remember that because it really resonated with me. I had a surgery several years ago that was pretty serious and I remember how big of a deal it was to see my family again coming out of surgery."

The nurses got me ready, put me in the wheelchair, and Mom and Dad wheeled me down to the waiting room and I was able to hold the girls for the first time since the day of my accident.

Billie may have been a little scared at first. But Cambell was so little she doesn't remember.

Billie wanted to be a part of it somehow and wanted to help me out. From the very beginning, she would help me get a drink and things like that.

We have a picture of that moment. I truly feel like that was the moment in my mind where I really started to realize it was all going to be okay. Somehow it was going to work out.

Jenny says it was one of those special moments you'll never forget. It's one of her favorite pictures.

In all those pictures from those days I'm always smiling.

PEER MENTORS

"We bring peer mentors into the hospital so that our patients can hear from someone they can relate to; People who have been there and lived through it."

~Dr. Jeffrey Guy

A peer visitor named Andy came to my room in the burn unit at Vanderbilt and asked me about my story. Andy was missing a few fingers. I could tell he had been in some type of fire and had some skin grafts. He was one of the first guys I could relate to because he was actually living it too. Up until then I had been talking with family and friends or doctors and nurses who had seen it before but never lived it. That made a big impact on me.

I told Andy my story and asked him about his. He was a pilot for a lawyer who had his own plane. Andy used the plane one time and took his family on vacation. The motor blew, so he had to make an emergency landing. The plane caught on fire. He carried each of his daughters and his wife out of the burning plane but they all died from their injuries.

After telling me his story, he said, "You know, Jason, if it was not for my church family I wouldn't be here today." He went through a major depression. I remember thinking I just lost two hands; this guy lost his family.

I only talked to Andy that one time in the hospital, but he made such an impression on me that I'll never forget him and what that conversation meant to me.

Fast-forward a few years and Mom and Dad bought a condo in Nashville on the river. Seven or eight years later we're down there in Nashville and this guy came over and started talking to me. So he started telling me this story and said he used to have his own plane and he had hired a pilot to fly it and all of a sudden it clicked in my head and I said, "Wait a minute, are you talking about Andy?" It was the lawyer whom Andy flew for!

I told him Andy was the first guy who came to my room and talked with me. We've reconnected and now we're Facebook friends.

That's just one of the many, many stories that kept pushing me forward. It reminds me that God definitely has a plan for me. I believed it before my accident, and I believe it now.

When Andy came to talk to me, it was just another example of God taking care of me. That experience with Andy was a big reason I decided to become a peer mentor later on.

HUMOR IS THE BEST MEDICINE

"Jason uses humor to make people feel more comfortable. That's his way to make it seem like this is no big deal."
~JENNY

There were lots of ups and downs at Vanderbilt. It wasn't always depressing and somber. There was always something to pick me up.

There was a time when my uncle came into the room and saw me for the first time. You have to know my family to understand his sense of humor, but I thought this was hilarious. He drove down to see me and as soon as he walked in the hospital room the very first thing he said to me was, "Well, what'd ya say, Stubby?" in a really funny voice. There were some shocked looks in the room, but I just busted up laughing and said, "Oh, not much!"

But that's just him. He's the type of person who copes with things by being funny or cracking jokes to lighten the mood. It's his way of expressing his feelings. I knew what he meant because that was his way of saying that nothing had changed; he's still my uncle, I'm still his nephew, and we're still going to pick on each other. Just like always.

It was nice seeing someone else reassure me this wasn't that big of a deal.

I understood, but the poor nurse who overheard it sure didn't know what to think.

Jenny tells a similar story about the time a psychiatrist came into my room to do a mental evaluation on me. She recalls, "They asked Jason to count forward and backward from ten. Jason looked right at him and without missing a beat he said, 'I'm going to have a hard time with this because I don't have my fingers anymore, but I'll do my best.' The poor guy didn't know what to think. But that's just Jason being Jason."

You've got to laugh to break up the serious moments. It's helpful even when you are working on something as serious as recovering from trauma. I was lucky enough to work with hospital staff who were willing to laugh with me too. Mike Elam was one of those staff members. He was a burn care specialist at Vanderbilt, and we developed a great relationship. Mike will tell you himself:

"I was not on duty the night Jason came in, but I worked with him often the rest of the time he was with us. I remember getting debriefed on what had happened and seeing pictures of his wounds. It was pretty gnarly stuff.

"But the thing I remember most about Jason is his great attitude throughout the whole process. He never got down or depressed that I ever saw. A lot of trauma patients hit an emotional wall. Jason never did. He never fussed or cussed about any of it. He was a patient I always looked forward to because he was always cutting up with people, and I liked that about him.

"I always tell people I had the honor and privilege of making Jason's first prosthetic hand for him.

"What happened was I was wheeling him back to his room and we decided to have some fun. So I took one of my surgical gloves and stuffed it full of paper towels so it actually took shape. Then we stuck it up Jason's hoodie sleeve. We did it to freak Jenny out, more or less. But then Jason started high-fiving and shaking hands with people in the hallway when I was wheeling him through the ICU floor and people got a kick out of that. Or he would wave and say, 'Hey, how do you like my new hand?'

"That was a good day. Just to get some smiles and laughs out of people was nice.

"But what was even better than that was the time we rigged up a way for him to feed himself. He was frustrated trying to eat. Caleb, one of the occupational therapists, was standing there, so the three of us started brainstorming. We taped a plastic spoon to his residual limb with some Medipore surgical tape. And it worked! He could feed himself. It's amazing what three rednecks can come up with! I guess you could say I made his first prosthetic device too.

"I always enjoyed talking with Jason when I was changing his bandages or whatever. We still keep in touch. I'm actually a little jealous of him because he has shot bigger deer with two fake arms than I have with normal arms."

MY ATTITUDE WAS MY DECISION

"I remember Dr. Guy explaining that Jason would go through depression. It was expected. It was normal. But they didn't understand Jason."
~JENNY

Dr. Guy told me about this one patient. She left the hospital clinically depressed. Eventually her husband left her. Her kids left her. She got a huge settlement from a car manufacturer because a defect had caused her accident. That still didn't lift her depression. Then one day he saw her and she was just vibrant. Smiling again. She told him that she just one day flipped a switch and realized she was not going to let her injuries keep her from enjoying life. When Dr. Guy was telling me about this woman's outlook changing, he explained it like her turning point was my starting point. He continues:

"Physical wounds heal in time. The emotional ones are tougher to heal sometimes.

"Jason didn't go through the normal cycle of depression. Instead, he was able to embrace his situation and started to put his life back together. Initially we thought Jason's attitude was an act. An appearance. That he was fine on the outside but crying on the inside. We were worried about that. We wanted him to know if he was crying on the inside, that's okay. It's normal. We'd get him help and it wouldn't last forever.

"We had a little bit of concern too that Jason's dad was this big, strong guy and we didn't want him or anyone in the family to be dismissive of those problems with a 'just buck up' attitude or 'just keep your chin up' or any of that cliché crap. This was major trauma. We wanted this to be seen as a problem for professionals to be handled by professionals and not just beaten with a positive attitude.

"Eventually we realized that was just Jason's normal attitude and it wasn't an act. But statistically, what happens in the family setting down the road is usually divorce, separation, depression, alcoholism, addiction, and suicide. We were anticipating all of those to come into play. Real, identified clinical issues. With Jason, they just never came.

"Body image is always an issue too. Particularly with men. They're used to being the caretaker, now others are taking care of them. Men have such an identity with their occupation. Jason was a construction worker, hunter, he was racing cars. It's easy to get into a downward spiral.

"Again, you can save somebody's life, but if you're not watching for all this stuff, you can do a huge disservice to the patient."

But the other thing Dr. Guy recognized is that I had a strong and compassionate family backing me. Their support was going to be important to my continued recovery back home and he could see that. He talks about his impression of them:

"Jason's obviously an amazing part of the story, but really his whole family is so much a part of his story.

"Now, having met the family, it's like they say, the apple doesn't fall far from the tree. The personality we met first in the hospital was Jason's dad. Mike is always up. Always kind. Always optimistic. I can see now where Jason gets it.

"I mean, Mike was taking care of the staff! Checking in on us and asking how we were doing. It was amazing.

"Sometimes it's easier for medical staff if the family hates us. It might sound strange. But for us, it helps to be distant. It's for our own self-protection. You have those moments when you have to tell a parent their child died from a motor vehicle accident and they start screaming and throwing chairs or something. That's normal. They don't want you around. So sometimes for us it's easier to expect the family to be distant and angry at us because of the situation. It's much more difficult when they're sweet and kind because it's almost like a discord. It's not what you expect. They should be angry.

"But the Kogers just weren't like that."

LEAVING THE HOSPITAL

"To see all those nurses and doctors cheering and clapping, some of them were crying, it was unbelievable. But Jason just had that kind of connection with all of them."
~MIKE KOGER

Dr. Guy will be the first to tell that he didn't feel great about letting me go home after just 12 days. He says: "We just didn't have a reason to keep him any longer. We had done everything we could medically. At that point it was really up to Jason if he was going to heal the rest of the way."

The hospital recommended that I go to rehab and do therapy at a place in Nashville. The first problem was that my family would only be able to see me twice a week, and it was a two- hour drive. My mom and dad went to go look at the place. Dad said it was a really old building and it was making him depressed just looking at it, so that wasn't going to do. They talked with Jenny and made a decision right then to take me home to Owensboro.

Dad says: "We went back and told them we were going to take him home and figure out a plan and do it ourselves. I feel like if he had gone there, he would have slipped into a depression and we didn't want that. We thought he'd be better off at home where he could be with his wife and kids and have us by his side too."

Of course, he was right. Being separated from my family and going through therapy alone wouldn't have worked for me.

Instead, the hospital began checking the Owensboro community to see what support was available there. Dr. Guy pulled my family aside to tell them that they expected there to be problems when I got home. Both emotionally and psychologically.

Dr. Guy said: "We didn't want that to be seen as pathological. We considered it normal. We wanted to get him help whenever that happened. And it most likely would happen. What's unique to Jason is there are people who are going to win at this and people who are going to lose when they're hurt this badly. There's really no in between. With some people, you're concerned they're going to give up and die. So when a patient leaves the burn unit you're wondering which one they will be. You just never know what you have in front of you."

There were the physical care requirements too. Jenny had to learn how to take care of my wounds. Before they released me, the nurse taught Jenny how to change my bandages and not cross-contaminate. She recalled:

"I had to wrap both arms, of course, but also skin grafts on his legs. So, I had to learn how to wash his wounds and bandage them but I couldn't use the same wash rag for his legs and arms. They had to be different because they didn't want to cross-contaminate. Then I had to wrap his leg with an Ace bandage from his hip to his ankle to keep compression on it."

I spent about 12 days total in the hospital. Three of those I was sedated. But it was time to go home and I was ready. The staff had one final surprise waiting for me as I was about to leave.

I never realized how many nurses, doctors, and students were watching me because I was just doing all this for myself.

I was told to expect to be there for months, but Dr. Guy released me in 12 days. So when he released me, they got me set up in the wheelchair and got me ready to go.

If you can picture this in your mind, the hallways in the burn unit are shaped like an "L" and my room was #3, which was on the short side. As they were wheeling me out, when they took me around the corner to the long hallway, both sides of the hallway were lined with nurses, doctors, residents, everybody shoulder to shoulder up and down both hallways clapping as they wheeled me out.

That was a huge pick-me-up for me. That was an unbelievable feeling. I felt like they were cheering me on the whole time actually, but especially in the final moment as they were saying goodbye and I was heading home.

Dr. Guy had a parting comment on my leaving: "When I think about this book, I think what readers need to understand is that I believe Jason chose his outcome. Yeah, he's from a good family, but I've seen people from good families still get totally jacked up. I think he chose in his mind how this was going to turn out for him.

"There are people with the same exact injuries Jason sustained who quit trying and eventually gave up. I don't think he sees himself as a victim from the injury. I'm sure Jason had dark hours. But I think he chose that he was going to win.

"I think I saw that thought process after Mike stepped out of his room that day Jason woke up.

"I truly believe that steely stare I saw in that first ten minutes determined the next ten years of his life."

CHAPTER 8

COMING HOME

*"At that point in my life, I was helping
Jenny the best I could with two young girls,
I didn't have time to feel sorry for myself."*
~Jason

The one thing that everybody has in common is that we all go through struggles.

It doesn't do much good to compare my struggles to your struggles or anybody else's because we all have our own. But we also have the same opportunity to overcome our struggles regardless of how big or how small they seem at the time.

For me, it came down to my faith in God, the hard work ethic my parents always taught me, our community's support, and my family and friends. But most especially Jenny. She went from my wife to my caretaker until I was back in a good routine. Through it all we stayed friends and I would say we're closer now than we've ever been. It was tough, though.

Jenny could have easily said, "I'm 27 years old. I don't want this life. I'm out!" But she didn't. We both believe marriage is worth fighting for.

I'll never forget this one time a lady sent me a Facebook message and told me that she and her husband were talking about getting a divorce. But after hearing our story and seeing what Jenny and I went through, they realized what they were going through was not that big of a deal. Just realizing that helped turn their marriage around. Hearing stories like that is a reminder of the importance of my marriage and looking out for my family.

I understand the concern early on that I would get depressed and lose hope. I get it.

Maybe I'm just that one person in a million to take it the way I took it, but I honestly believe it was because I did not have time to worry about myself. I had a wife and two little girls to keep my mind occupied.

You know how it is with small kids; there weren't five idle minutes in the day for me to sit around and be sad and depressed. I had one crying. One hungry. One needing a diaper changed that I'd hand off to Jenny. I might have needed to get to therapy in five minutes, or head to the ball field on the way back from my appointment. It was always something! We were always coming and going.

It's been busy since the day we got home up until today. It hasn't really ever slowed down.

That's just the way our lives are. It's never, "Take your time, you got 30 minutes." It seems like it's always, *"Hurry up! You're going to be late if you don't leave right now!"*

Now that I see how it's all turned out, I can see how if I had been older when it happened and the kids were out of the house, or if I was younger and single, I don't know how I would have reacted. Especially that first year or two.

But at that point in my life, helping Jenny the best I could with two young girls, I didn't have time to feel sorry for myself.

My faith had a lot to do with it, sure. But being a dad and husband was most of it, I think. I was too busy to ever sit back and think, *Why did this happen to me?* Because every time I had a minute to sit and those thoughts crept in I'd have a kid come run

and jump in my lap or climb up on the couch and want to read a book or something. I think that was the best therapy for me, really. (I have a YouTube video that a local church made in 2009 that I use to show people my testimony. Just google "Jason Koger Story" and you'll see it.)

Those first two years after my accident I was never left alone. Married. Two kids. Family. I had somebody with me all the time. I think putting yourself in a position where you're around people who care about you is a big part of recovery.

Everybody needs somebody.

WELCOME HOME

"People brought us meals for months. A lady who went to our church cleaned our house once a week for free. Those kinds of things meant so much. God always took care of us."

~JENNY

That first day driving back to Owensboro from Nashville, we saw the coolest thing. Just about a mile from our house, we drove past Panther Creek Baptist Church. They had written "Welcome Home, Jason" on their sign out front.

We don't even go to church there. But someone thought enough to call ahead and tell them we were coming home and they took the time to put that up on their marquee. Those small things like that meant so much to me and my family.

This community did so much. It was truly amazing. People were putting together fundraiser events. Others were bringing us meals every night. Somebody went through the effort to organize that and took the time to cook those meals for us.

So many things.

The CaringBridge that Toby set up for us was still getting messages like crazy for the longest time.

Things like that helped me stay positive. Just seeing all that support felt like riding a wave, like being picked up and carried. Any time I struggled, I knew in the back of my mind that support was there.

We had a lot of support, and we needed it. Those were tough times. Jenny remembers:

"People have said they couldn't believe I didn't leave Jason. But that's not me. I said I would be in this with him. For better or for worse. Whatever life brings. In sickness and in health. Richer or poorer. We've been all of those. We were on food stamps for a while about six months after his accident. He wasn't working, obviously, and I lost my job. We had no income for a while, so we were on food stamps for like six months. It was so humbling. But you have to do what you have to do.

"I remember one time I was literally sitting there wondering how we were going to pay our bills that month and a lady from where I worked came by, knocked on the door, and said her church Sunday school class decided to pay our electric bill that month.

"If you weren't looking for it, you could look right by that and not notice, but I knew that was God working. That's not a coincidence. God was totally getting us from this point to that point to this next point until finally, we were okay.

"The way God orchestrated it all, you couldn't even dream it. It was just one unexpected blessing after another. It was like, now we'll be okay for a little bit longer. And a little bit longer. From this point to that point."

That's why I feel like we live in one of the best places in the country. There are definite benefits that come along with being from a small town. The whole community sent us so much help that all I had to do was focus on getting better. We didn't have to worry about food or bills or cleaning house for those first months. We'll be forever grateful to Owensboro. And I'm so humbled. Which is one of the reasons I feel so strongly about giving back.

None of this stuff that's happened since 2008 would have happened if it wasn't for that support from Owensboro those first few months.

FRIENDS AND FAMILY CAME TOGETHER

"That first year after Jason's accident, it was seriously like taking care of three kids, with a two-year-old, a three-month-old, and a husband that needed me to care for him too. Looking back, I honestly don't know how I did it, but we made it through."

~JENNY

[As told by Jenny Koger]

There was Cambell, our sweet little baby in the middle of all this. Bless her heart, her first year was such a blur. With Cambell we just couldn't be as attentive as we were with Billie Grace when she was a baby. That's probably why she's such an independent, free-spirited kid.

I also couldn't leave Cambell alone with Billie for very long because Billie would pick Cambell up like a baby doll. But I still had to give Jason a bath, too. Sometimes I felt like I didn't even have time to go to the bathroom myself.

Some days I'd give all three of them a bath and then be too exhausted to even give myself a bath by that point. It was physically exhausting at times.

But then in the middle of it all, I also remember one of Jason's friends called and said they were going to sit with the kids and visit with Jason so I could go out for a while and just have a break. That meant so much just knowing that they were considerate of how it was affecting me. That was such a thoughtful thing to do. It inspired me to think outside the box a little more and think of ways to be more thoughtful to others since then.

Another time, one of our friend's mom sent me some money in a card and she told me to do something nice for myself. I don't even remember what I used the money for. I probably went to the mall just to get a way for a little while. What I remember is how much her consideration meant to me. There were people constantly checking in on us and taking care of us in thoughtful ways like that.

Jason's dad, Mike, also recalled a great giving moment from a friend:

"We had a friend ask what he could do to help, besides give money. He wanted to help in a meaningful way.

"One thing somebody had mentioned is that Jason would be better off with levered door handles instead of regular door knobs because they'd be easier to turn with his prosthetic hands. So my friend had somebody come and change all the doorknobs in Jason and Jenny's house to levers.

"Things like that meant so much. Those are things you'll never forget.

"Today, we have levers on all the doors at our house and all our rental properties so Jason can get around a little easier."

Of course, we continued to receive strong support from our families. Even Jason's aunt who lives two houses down would come over to sit with the girls while I changed Jason's bandages. When I finally went back to work, Jason's sister, Holly, babysat for us. She and I have always been close. Billie Grace actually helped a lot too, even though she was just under two years old. She helped me a lot. There were times it was just too much. I felt like I couldn't breathe. Like I was drowning. I took any help I could get.

I can remember going to bed and praying that God would give me strength for tomorrow. My brain couldn't focus on two days, or tomorrow. I just needed to focus on one day at a time.

I'd pray, "Just for today, Lord." I have to keep these two little people alive and Jason needs me to do so much for him, too.

Donna still thinks about the first year's struggles, but she also talks about how blessed they were.

"There were so many things that remind me how blessed we all are. In October, after his accident, Jason and Jenny went to a conference for bilateral upper limb amputees in Colorado called 'Enhancing Skills for Life' and I went along with them. That was a real eye-opener to me. It was all still so new to us and we were still figuring all this out.

"When we got to the conference that first night, as other amputees and people with other disabilities started coming in it almost felt strange. It still was hard to grasp that this was our new reality.

"I'll never forget Jenny looked over and saw a woman who was born without arms and she was using her feet to take a drink. So it was just that realization that things could be so much worse. But all these people were getting along just fine. One way or another.

"During this conference, they had a workshop for caretakers that Jenny and I went to. We had Billie Grace and Cambell with us, so I was sort of in and out of the conference so Jenny could hear everything herself.

"At one point there was this lady telling Jenny that her problem was her son was so angry. He was angry at the world, and even angry at her sometimes. I believe he was in a car accident and lost several limbs. She had to take him upstairs, and it was difficult, and he would curse and throw things because he was just so angry all the time.

"When Jenny was telling me that, I can remember thinking how blessed we are that Jason doesn't have that anger. He could have taken on that same attitude and been taking it out on the people that love him. It could have turned out totally different. We are very blessed."

Fortunately, I got really lucky because my in-laws are great. I have people all the time make comments about how odd it is that we vacation together and go to the lake together and all this when most people's in-laws get on their nerves.

I think it really helped that we were close before. I've known Mike and Donna since I was 19 and we've always been close so I was super comfortable with them by then. We've always done

a lot with them. We always had Sunday dinner with them and typically still do.

There was no awkwardness or friction when it came to caregiving for Jason after his accident. It's just what needed to happen. Donna offered, and she didn't overstep. I was willing to take all the help I could get. Donna and I made a pretty good team. She helped a lot.

Donna says: "It was like this back-and-forth, mother and wife. Sometimes it did take both of us, and not just one person. Together, Jenny and I made a good team, because Jenny would have been overwhelmed sometimes and I would have babied him to death.

"Again, it was like God just giving us exactly what we needed. Putting all those pieces together. As the months went on and Jason got better at things, there were certain things where Jenny would say, 'Now, Donna. You've got to let him do it. He's got to learn to do it on his own.' And I'd want to say, 'No, he needs help.' I wanted to help him so bad. It's just that motherly instinct."

Mike had some thoughts about that time as well: "When Jason got home, he would call on Donna sometimes to come out and give Jenny a hand. Donna used to be a nurse so she and Jenny shared changing his bandages. Jenny was a bit squeamish at first, but she got used to it. "No mom would ever imagine giving her 29-year-old son a shower, but that's what Donna had to do and she did it.

Same way with Jenny. Just gotta do what you gotta do."

There were some lighter moments that we could laugh at though. I can remember one time when I was trying to potty train Billie and I told Jason that I just needed to get out and go for a walk. I rarely got a moment to myself and I just needed a minute. So, I walked up the lane to just take a break and get some fresh air.

When I walked back in the house, Billie looked at me and said, "Momma, don't ever leave me here with Daddy again. Dad tried to wipe my butt with him's hooks."

That's how she said it, *"Him's hooks."* We got such a good laugh out of that.

Just like when Jason says the girls and I were his motivation; well, he and the girls were my motivation, too.

If we didn't have kids, I think maybe it would have been harder. But it was this feeling like I *have* to do this. I don't have a choice. The girls were part of my reason to take care of him. And taking care of him was also me taking care of them. We're in this together. It wasn't just about me and Jason. It was about our family.

If Jason needed me in the bathroom, but Cambell's crying at the same time, and then Billie Grace is getting into something or

pouring something out on the floor or doing whatever toddlers do, I had to prioritize. Sometimes Jason got sick of waiting. But in those moments, he was forced to learn to do some things on his own. Whereas if he had been in a care facility or not been married and living with his mom or something, then he would have gotten one-on-one attention and it would have been instantly done because that's a mother's instinct. But that wasn't our reality.

In his situation, it was the life he had here at home that enabled him to be in situations where he had to figure certain things out. It was a necessity.

So having two young kids and eventually a third dependent was tough. But it was also our motivation. Our higher priority.

Still, taking on the caregiver role was a tough transition. Jason's independent, and he tried hard that first year. But he just

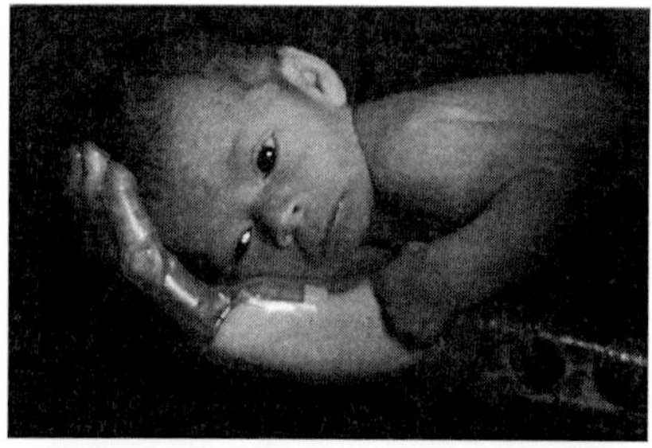

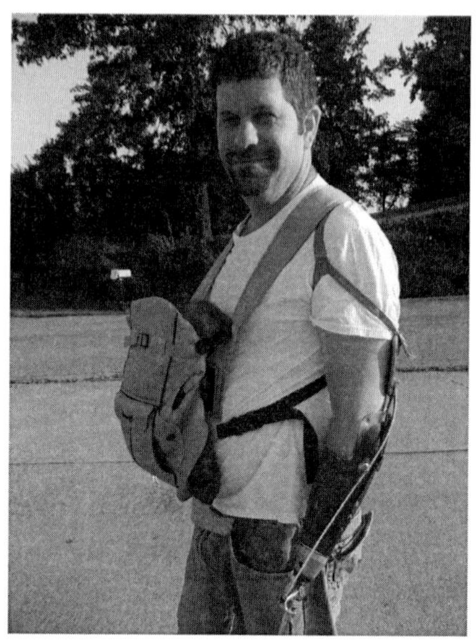

couldn't do things by himself. Slowly, though, he learned how.

I don't remember when I stopped having to help him go to the bathroom. It wasn't overnight, that's for sure.

Nobody wants to do that. When you go from a wife to a caregiver, it changes the dynamic of your marriage. It was really, really hard. You have to remember, we had only been married three and a half years when he had his accident.

Looking back, this made us both stronger. It made Jason stronger. It made me stronger. It made our marriage stronger.

But there were some tough times. We had our struggles. There were times when our marriage was not really a marriage because I was a caregiver more than a wife.

Over time, and the more independent Jason got, the more I had the time to be on my own and decompress. We didn't lose what we had for each other because we fought for our marriage and kept it a priority through that hard time.

Eventually, we made it through. The whole dynamic changed over time and three years later we were ready to have another baby and we did.

Having Axell was another miracle because they told us that because of the electricity we would likely not be able to have any more kids. But here we are. It worked out just fine.

I keep saying that God always gave us that next step, whatever we needed at the time. We wanted another child, and God gave us Axell.

NEVER AGAIN

"I remember one of my lowest moments when it hit me so hard how much my life had changed forever."
~JASON

[As told by Jason]

It was the first week I was home. I was sitting on the couch. No arms. No prostheses yet. And Billie Grace came in the room and crawled up on the couch and lay down next to me with her head in my lap and raised her arm up in the air.

She used to do that a lot because when I had hands, I would always run my fingers down her ribcage and act like I was counting her ribs and tickle her. It was just a silly thing we always did.

That time she did it out of habit. I looked down and she was looking up at me and I could tell she was expecting me to tickle her ribs. It just hit me so hard that I couldn't do that anymore.

I had to play it off in the moment and I don't remember now what I said, but it was bedtime so Jenny and I put her to bed.

A few minutes after we told her good night and closed the door, I completely broke down and cried. It was one of the few times I did that. But it just killed me realizing I couldn't do those little things anymore.

Jenny came into the living room and found me crying and said, "What in the world is wrong?" I told her that was something I'm going to miss. Something that simple.

Well actually, I can do it now. Just not the same way. But that night, not knowing what my future would hold, I thought I would never be able to do that again.

HOBBY LOBBY

"I have no idea how many people saw me waddling across that store because all I could think about was getting to Jenny as fast as I could."

~JASON

There were so many funny times with the kids. I tell this story almost every time I give a speech because it was the funniest thing ever and it always gets a good laugh. Though it was pretty embarrassing for me at the time.

It was our first trip to town as a family after my accident. I was getting a little stir-crazy and we had loaded up and headed into town to run a few errands. Jenny needed something from Hobby Lobby so we all went inside together.

Jenny took Cambell because she was only three months old. Jenny put her in the shopping cart and I took Billie with me to go walk around. Billie Grace was around 21 months old.

Billie and I were walking up and down the aisles. Not in any hurry. We weren't shopping for anything in particular, just sort of passing the time.

This was before I had my prostheses so I was carrying her but she asked me to put her down. When I did, she started running away from me so I yelled out, "Billie Grace, get back over here." Loud enough to get her attention but not loud enough for the whole store to hear.

She came back to me, but when she did, she turned around and gave me this big grin.

From my perspective, it turned into one of those moments like you see in movies where everything turns to slow motion.

She ran to me with her arms out so of course I thought it was going to be this big, special moment where she jumps up in my arms and we give each other a big hug.

But instead, she grabbed me by my pants and pulled my pants all the way down to my ankles. I was wearing athletic shorts with an elastic waist so they were easy to slide down. Fortunately, my underwear stayed up. But she got me good!

And I couldn't pull 'em up because I didn't have arms.

There I was, standing there in the store with my pants down to my ankles and Billie's still grinning at me while I'm yelling, "Billie, pull up my pants!" She just stood there grinning. I had to waddle three aisles over to find Jenny so she could pull my pants back up for me. Kids. I tell ya!

Those are some of the things that got us through that first year after my accident. There were highs and lows. But we kept moving forward.

I got hurt March 1st and my last surgery was December 5th, which was another skin graft. Then there was therapy and prosthetic fittings the next few years.

I'm still learning every day, but those first two years were the roughest. It gradually got easier.

Eventually, Dr. Guy got his wish: I got my life back.

CHAPTER 9

BACK IN THE WOODS

*"After a couple tries, I found out I could hold
a crossbow with one prosthetic arm."*
~JASON

My number one goal of holding my girls again was followed by getting home and getting back to regular life. I wanted to get back into the woods and hunt as soon as I could. It was the next thing I needed to do to start feeling normal again.

It happened a lot sooner than I expected.

I like deer hunting a lot. But turkey hunting is just so much fun because of the way you have to interact with those birds. Calling them in is a real challenge. (For people who don't hunt,

that is using turkey sounds to get their attention.) You've got to work for it.

Sam Smith was one of my best hunting buddies long before my accident. I met Sam while working with him as a pipefitter. He invited me to Butler County, which is about 60 miles south of Owensboro, to go hunting with him.

I ended up buying a farm right next to his land in Butler County and we'd both hunt on each other's land down there.

Sam got hurt falling out of a deer stand about a year before my accident. He ended up breaking his back. It's ironic that he was also life-flighted to Vanderbilt after his accident. I remember going down to the hospital to see him and tried to be there for him. When he got back to the woods again, we'd go hunting together with our crossbows. I wasn't so much there to hunt for myself. Instead, it was more about being with him while he got back to hunting again.

When my accident happened, Sam showed up at the hospital and was there pretty much the whole time. When I got home, he told me more than once that he was going to make sure that I got back to hunting again.

Sam talks about our history as friends:

"I worked for Jason's dad, Mike, when Jason got out of college. Mike told me to break Jason in so I rode him pretty hard for the first two weeks.

"One time, before he lost his hands, we were welding up on this 125 ft lift. He was holding this piece of metal on this tank and I was welding it. It was a hot day. We were both dripping with sweat, so when I struck that welder, it would shock him a little bit. But he couldn't drop it because there were people working underneath us. He tells everybody I was the first person to electrocute him.

"Like Jason said, I was hanging deer stands about 22 feet in the air when the strap holding me broke. I fell and broke my back. Jason and his family were right there for me.

"I remember coming home the day Jason got hurt to my wife telling me he was shocked by a downed power line. I told her that there was no way that could be true because nobody was working that day. I didn't understand yet that it didn't happen at work. I headed to Nashville as fast as I could and stayed right there by his side.

"I was in the hospital the entire time leading up to when he became conscious again. Other than family, I was one of the first people in the room. Everybody kept telling me not to break down when I was in the room with Jason. Well, that was hard to do. The first thing he asked me after he woke up was, 'How am I going to pull my bow back?'

"That hit me pretty hard. Even though I tried to be strong. I know my lip was quivering. But I just looked him in the eyes and said, 'Jason, I don't know. But we're going to do everything we've always done. We'll just do it a little bit differently.'

"That's exactly what we did."

I got hurt in March and turkey season opens in April. That April, Sam called me and said, "Hey, I'm going to take you turkey hunting." I said sure, but I was really just thinking I'd go sit in the woods and watch him while he hunted. I didn't even have prostheses yet. I was fine with watching. I just wanted to get back out there again.

I didn't think I'd ever be able to hunt again because I didn't realize then how advanced the field of prosthetics had become and how much prostheses allowed amputees to do. It was so early on that I wasn't even worried about hunting at the time.

I called my doctor and asked him if I could go hunting and Dr.

Guy said he didn't see any reason I shouldn't. That's all I needed to hear. I went down to Sam's place and spent the night so we could get up early and go hunting that next morning.

That night, Sam and I were sitting up talking and he said, "You're hunting tomorrow. We're going to figure this out." I said okay but, in my mind, I was really thinking he must be out of his mind!

The next thing I know he took a shotgun there in the living room, took the two screws out of the butt of the shotgun where it rests on your shoulder, slid a ratchet strap under it, ran the screws back through it, and strapped the gun to my shoulder by slipping the strap under my armpit, around my back, over my other shoulder, and tightened it down so the gun stayed snug against my right shoulder.

Then he took a tripod and a radiator hose clamp and strapped the shotgun to the tripod so the barrel could point in the air. That gave me just a little bit of range.

He figured that part might work, but the next problem was pulling the trigger.

To solve that, Sam tied a string to the trigger and stuck the end of that string in my mouth so all I had to do was jerk my head to the side and the trigger would fire.

If you can picture this, imagine me sitting on the ground with my back up against a tree. I had that shotgun ratchet strapped to my shoulder, balanced on the tripod, with that string in my mouth, just sitting there waiting.

If a turkey came up behind me, I would have no shot. The only range of motion I had was to lean a little bit to one side or rotate my shoulders just enough to pivot that shotgun on the tripod a teeny bit side to side. It was actually not a whole lot different than how some turkey hunters will sit against a tree and rest the gun on one knee. Except I didn't have arms to move the gun up and down. I could only move side to side. A turkey would have to walk through that tiny little window of opportunity in order for me to have a shot.

It seemed impossible.

But sure enough, the next day we were out hunting and Sam started calling (with his turkey call). We heard a turkey gobble back and it wasn't very far away at all.

Where we were sitting there was a little creek with a little dirt game trail right on the other side. Sam said he thought that turkey might come right down through there. So, I got myself ready and leaned up tight against that tree and waited.

Pretty soon a hen (female) walked past and I could barely see a jake (male) coming down through that game trail behind her. I remember sitting there, not moving a muscle except my eyes back and forth because a turkey can see motion really well. You have to move very slowly, if at all, because their eyesight is so keen, they can see your eyes blink.

You've got to be camouflaged, almost indistinguishable, and stay perfectly still. I was trying to stay relaxed and not get too excited because with my eyes angled toward that turkey, I could see there was a chance he could come into my little shooting zone.

Once he was finally in that zone, he kept moving and ended up pretty much on-center. It was then that I took the shot and dropped him.

It was the best feeling in the world!

Sam and I were both hootin' and hollerin'! It was unbelievable! Sam's plan totally worked, against all odds.

It used to be I'd kill two turkeys a year. When I had hands, as you can imagine, it was a whole lot easier because you can pull up, follow the bird, and shoot. But with this ratchet strap concoction, it had to be lined up perfectly and there was still a very small chance.

The rest of that year was a disaster. I missed so many birds that season. But the one I did kill made it all worth it.

My other buddy Lance Chapman, whom I hunt with a lot too, was actually telling people I was on a shoot and release program that year.

Sam recalls a hunting story with the three of us:

"Lance was with us the day of the mysterious disappearing turkey.

"On that particular day it seemed like everything was going wrong. I can't tell you how many turkeys we called in that day, but they all got away. Finally, I told Koger we were about to run out of land so he'd better get one real quick.

"Lance was filming all of this, so we have it on video. Jason finally got one lined up and knocked it down. It looked like it was laying there graveyard dead. All three of us were jumping and screaming and hugging and high-fiving each other because we were so happy Jason got another one.

"Eventually we calmed down and rolled the film back to watch. But when we walked back in the field to get it, the turkey was gone! It had gotten up and run off! With all our celebrating, we hadn't even noticed that the bird somehow survived that shot and got up and ran away.

"We tracked it like a deer, but it must have lived through it and run away. We never did find that bird."

There's another cool story I like to tell about my buddy Lance. He was hunting with Drury Outdoors one year when they did this thing called "Dream Season with Celebrities." What they did was match people from Drury Outdoors with celebrities for a fundraiser for children's hospitals. At the end of the season, they took one of those terminally ill kids hunting with a celebrity.

Lance was paired up with Adam Wainwright, who is a pitcher for the St. Louis Cardinals. Lance and Adam hunted in several states and became pretty good friends. I remember Lance telling me how special it was for him and Adam to take one of the kids hunting knowing that it might be that kid's last chance to be in the woods. After they were done with the hunt the next day, Lance said he and Adam just sat there and cried like babies. They were looking back on their Dream Season and talking about how special it was to make a good memory for that kid. Part of it was realizing there are so many people going through hard times like that. That story just goes to show what kind of guy Lance is.

I also met and hunted with Buddy Owens. He's known for hunting as well as his music career as a songwriter for people like Blake Shelton and Miranda Lambert and several others.

I've met so many awesome people in the hunting world. Lance and Sam are two of the guys who helped me get back in the woods after my accident. I'll forever be grateful to them for that.

DEER SEASON

"Eventually, I got comfortable enough to where I could hunt on my own again. I'll never forget that first year hunting again with Sam, though."

~JASON

When deer season rolled around in October, that first fall after my accident, I had my left arm prosthetic. But I didn't have my right arm yet because it needed more surgeries. After a couple tries, though, I found out I could hold a crossbow with one prosthetic arm.

I could hold the crossbow and aim, but I only had one hand, so it was so much easier for Sam to pull the trigger for me. Sam and I came up with a system where I'd get it lined up and tell Sam when I was center. Then Sam would reach around and pull the trigger. It was a tag-team situation, but it worked out. That's how I, or actually we, killed my first deer that season, a button buck (a male fawn six months of age or younger).

I ended up killing several deer those first couple years. But I'll never forget the story of one deer in particular. Sam and I saw it but couldn't really tell how far it was from us.

With a crossbow, there are three or four pins in the scope to help you gauge distance. Sam suggested I use my top pin. So, I did, but when I took the shot it went right over the deer's back. I switched to the bottom pin and shot but it went right underneath its belly. He just stood there.

Lastly, Sam said, "Use the middle pin, you'll kill it." I did and finally dropped him. Third time's the charm, right?

Sam has stories to tell too.

"Of course, any time Jason missed that first year, that meant he could somehow blame me. Now, you tell me if this makes any sense to you," he says, grinning.

"That first deer season after his accident, we went hunting together like we usually did. After we got our one-arm-each system worked out, we finally saw a doe and Koger had it lined up in the scope. Then he told me, 'All right, I'm on her. Pull it.'

"I did as he asked, but the shot went straight over her back. And he looked up at me and said, dead serious, 'You missed!'

"I said, 'Dude, what do you mean, I missed? All I did was pull the trigger.' Then he said, 'No. You jerked the trigger. You didn't pull it.'

"It took us three attempts but we finally killed it. We were dying laughing. Some of the stuff we've had happen when we're hunting is just hilarious.

"But seriously, our stories are great but they aren't the most important takeaway here. What's most important to know is that Jason's will to overcome and get on with life is remarkable. From the day he got out of the hospital he has never looked back and never stopped going forward. He's just determined and stops at nothing."

Eventually, I got comfortable enough to where I could hunt on my own again. I'll never forget that first year hunting again with Sam, though.

It all started with his MacGyver maneuver with that ratchet-strapped shotgun. I still laugh about it because I honestly didn't think I was going hunting that day. I thought I was just going to sit with him while he hunted. But Sam was determined to make it happen, and I'm so thankful he did.

My record hunts wouldn't come until much later, when I had my prostheses fitted right and was more comfortable hunting by myself. But that was all made possible when Sam helped me get my first turkey.

My friend Danny Jarboe was another buddy who took me turkey hunting in those early years after my accident and helped me get back to doing what I really love to do.

Looking back now as I'm writing this, it also makes me even more appreciative of all my friends like Danny Jarboe, Jeff Jacobs (whom you'll hear about later), Sam Smith, Lance Chapman, and others who not only took me hunting, but sometimes let me hunt on their land. I mention that because these days hunting has gotten so big and so competitive that most people are secretive and protective of good hunting spots. It seems like hunting has become all about the money for a lot of people. Now farmers know they can rent their land for hunting privileges. So, it means a lot to me that these guys took me with them and got me back out hunting again. Sometimes they even took me on *their* land to hunt the deer and turkeys that they themselves had been tracking. That's a very gracious and unselfish thing to do.

These guys did that at a crucial point for me. It was at a time when I was trying to figure out if I could even hunt again. Did I even want to? Would my passion die? Should I just give it up as one more thing I couldn't do anymore and let it go?

But because of my great friends, my passion for hunting didn't die. It actually grew! So much so that I still take my own kids hunting today. I'm so thankful for those times. Then, and now.

THE BIONIC MAN

*"I have to make a decision every day when I
wake up in the morning which set of arms to put
on based on what I have going on that day."*
~JASON

Because I was 29 when I lost my hands, I remember how certain things feel, like what a steering wheel feels like in your hand or sliding on a pair of leather gloves.

I also still remember how to do things with my hands, like change the oil in my truck, for example. Or use a screwdriver. It's really frustrating to me now because I know the normal way to

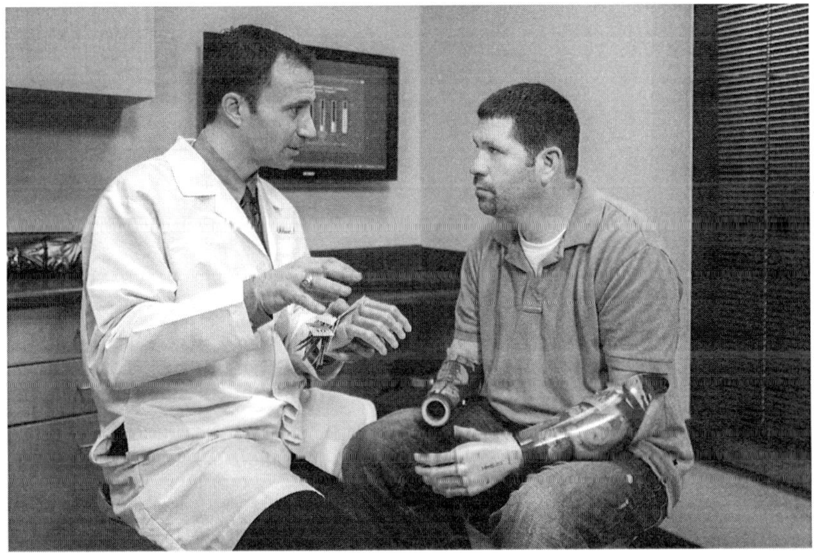

Photo courtesy of Advanced Arm Dynamics

do it and it was so much simpler. Now I've had to relearn how to do all those things. I can still do almost anything I could before, it just takes me longer now.

The most frustrating thing is when I'm trying to show my kids how to do something and I'm trying to tell them to put their hands a certain way. For instance, I know exactly how you put your fingers on a baseball or a fishing rod but I can't show them because I don't have hands. That's a killer.

That's something amputees struggle with that other people don't understand.

I remember getting aggravated at different things. Jenny is not mechanically inclined at all and it bugs the heck out of me. Sometimes I'll sit and watch her do things that I could do so much faster. But I have to wait and watch because she's still faster doing things her way than I am with bionics.

Or when I have to struggle to explain something that's so simple in my head but I can't explain it any better than repeating, "just line that nut up with those threads on that bolt and twist it down!" Something simple like that. Knowing how to do it in my mind and not being able to do it is so aggravating.

When I first got home there were lots of situations where I was trying to learn how to do certain things and I could visually see how to do something, but I just couldn't do it. That would burn me up!

Then when I did ask for help, I'd be asking for a tool by name and Jenny or the kids didn't know which tool I meant. So instead of just grabbing a wrench myself like I used to be able to, I had to say, "It's the red-handled tool in the second drawer that's shaped like a 'U' on the end."

The thing that helped me the most was somebody told me early on that no matter what, don't take it out on your family.

You're going to have difficulties and rough days and tough situations but don't take your frustration out on your family. When you get mad, go outside and kick rocks and walk around instead.

I can't tell you how many times I'd get frustrated doing something but I'd walk up to the barn and back and try again. There were lots of times I did that. I'd calm down and go at it again. I try really hard not to take it out on anybody around me.

THE RIGHT FIT

"We use a term called resiliency where we gauge someone's ability to overcome their situation and make something out of it. Jason is by far the most resilient person I've ever met."
~Rob Dodson, CPO (Certified Prosthetist Orthotist)

Getting the proper prostheses makes all the difference. That's a whole process in itself and it involves a lot of trial and error until you get the right fit. For me, finding the right prosthetist was crucial, so that's where I always tell other amputees to start.

Once my surgeries and skin grafts were finally done and healed up, I started trying to get fitted for prostheses.

Your arms change so much during the process because they shrink and your muscles change. The skin grafts have to heal. Scar tissue has to wear down and be desensitized.

That process involves therapy sessions multiple times a day. Hot wax, massages, and ultrasound. It takes all of that to break the scar tissue down so the prostheses fit the socket better and it won't hurt so much.

I was denied by insurance a few times for prosthetics, which was extremely hard to deal with. It's a long process, but once I got okayed, I got started with a prosthetist in Nashville. I had only a little bit of success. My first fit wasn't great. I didn't know the difference then so I wore them anyway because that's all I knew. It hurt to wear them all of the time though, so I didn't wear them a lot.

Most prosthetists are used to leg amputations, which apparently are a little easier to fit. But bilateral arm amputations are pretty rare, so it's a little more difficult to find a prosthetist with experience fitting upper limbs.

I was referred on to a prosthetist in Texas, and when I walked out of his office with my new fitted sockets, I could immediately feel the difference. My sockets immediately felt like a part of me and I wore them all day.

I remember walking through the airport feeling good. I made my way all the way home, still feeling good. That was the day things changed for me. From there, I was able to do even more and do more normal things again. I really started getting good at using my new arms once I was fit properly.

I always tell amputees to take their time to find a prosthetist you like because the right fit is everything. Your prostheses have to fit right to be successful, but what's even more important is finding the right fit with your prosthetist.

It truly takes a great team of multiple people to be successful as an amputee. My prosthetist is Rob Dodson with Arm Dynamics. Some insurance companies don't understand why a guy in Kentucky needs to go all the way to Texas for a prosthetist. But it's because in my opinion Rob is the best in the country. He and I fit. We're a team. I tell people when they become an amputee that you want that same level of confidence in your prosthetist because this is a relationship you're going to have for the rest of your life. You need to shop around and find out who's going to be the best fit for you. You don't want to be in a situation where your prosthetist isn't going to do you right.

I tell people to go talk to three different prosthetists. And also talk to three different companies. Then ask all three the exact same questions. That's how you find out who and what equipment works best for you.

You need confidence in your prosthetist. With Rob Dodson, I can call at any moment and get something done. If I break something, I overnight my arm to Texas and I know they're going to fix it as fast as they can and get it back to me because he understands that's my livelihood. That's what I need to have to be able to do what I do. When he's working with me, we talk about what I'm doing, what my goals are, and what my lifestyle is like. He takes his time with me because he wants to know as much as he can about the specifics of my life. That way we can make decisions together about what I need from my arms. Then he'll make it happen.

You always hear about doctors who rush patients through. But Rob and Arm Dynamics specialize in upper limb prosthesis and that's what he's best at. If he has an upper and lower, he'll just do the upper and refer the lower to another prosthetist. A lot of people wouldn't do that. They'd do it all and make a ton of money. Rob's not like that. He wants the best for his patients.

Not only that, but Arm Dynamics also has therapists on site. When you go in for a fitting, you're also working with a therapist to learn how to use the prosthesis most effectively and how to do things with it. Rob will basically build a prototype for me, then I work with an occupational therapist and use it a while. I tell them about my experience, where it hurts, and other things about using it. Then Rob circles that area on the prototype and works on it some more until it fits exactly right. It takes a while.

Sometimes almost a week. Because it's one-on-one with the pros-thetist and the therapist. It's not like an appointment for an hour. You're there as long as it takes.

When I leave, I know I've got something that's going to work exactly right and something I can wear and not start hurting thirty minutes after I leave. You hear so many examples of amputees whose protheses sit in a closet because they can't wear them. That's not how it is with Arm Dynamics. At least not in my experience with them.

Rob Dodson, my prosthetist and clinical manager at Arm Dynamics, explains it this way:

"Part of the magic with this job is you do develop long term relationships with people. You want a good relationship with your dentist or eye doctor but in those situations, you may spend fifteen or thirty minutes with them and you see them next time. With a prosthetic patient, we spend six hours with them, and in some cases, we schedule a whole week. Jason, for example, is coming back in a couple weeks and we've got him scheduled for five straight days. Prosthetics is about building long-term rela-tionships because we need to make sure that what we're fitting someone with is comfortable and functional.

"When we met Jason, for example, one of our prosthetists was at an amputee conference. At the time, Jason had been fitted by a local prosthetist. When Jason came in to meet us that first time, our closest office to him was in Dallas. He came out to see what the process was and to decide if it even made sense to travel that far. I told him that since he was here already, why not let me try a mold real quick to show him what a good fit was supposed to feel like. What he had at the time was a good attempt by somebody who doesn't do this a lot. We did an evaluation real quick and made up a socket he could slip his arm into and immediately he said it didn't hurt. He told me that his other prosthetist said he would get used to it and it wouldn't hurt eventually. I think that changed Jason's perspective.

"I don't fault other prosthetists though because upper limb amputees are so rare. About 90% of amputees are lower limb, because of injury or diabetes or whatever. Only about 10% are upper limb, and only a few of those are bilateral uppers like Jason. So, most prosthetists don't fit many arms because there's not a lot of cases out there. A prosthetist might fit thirty legs to one arm. The average prosthetist might fit two or three arms a year.

"But what our president decided to do when he started Arm Dynamics is focus on the 10% and we try to be 100% effective on that 10%. We only do arms here. We don't want to dilute our skills and try to be experts on uppers and lowers. We focus on uppers. I use all that experience on every patient that comes through our door.

"Yeah, our way of doing things means Jason has to travel to Dallas and spend a week. But that's compared to making multiple trips of a few hours' driving time back and forth over the course of several weeks. We just compress the time into one trip. It's a lot of time at once, but in the long run, it actually saves time.

"That's what started our journey together, and that is what I call it: a journey. With prosthetics, there's no end destination It just goes on. It's not like other surgeries where you heal and you're done. With prosthetics, there's always something breaking, there's always new technology, and patients' bodies change over time so we're constantly chasing a fit because there are a lot of variables that go into it. So, we have worked out a system that works well for people traveling from far away. I'd say about 60% of our patients come from over three hours away.

"We use a term called resiliency where we gauge someone's

ability to overcome their situation and make something out of it. Jason is by far the most resilient person I've ever met. He has taken what would cause most people to curl up in a fetal position on the couch and instead he's done some amazing things. He is so inspirational to others.

"I tell patients all the time that they will quickly transition from being a mentee to being a mentor. Meaning: they are going through something difficult right now that somebody else will soon be facing. Jason's great about being a mentor to other patients because he can commiserate and empathize, but he can also speak truth into that person's life and say, 'Hey, your life's not over. And I'm a good example of that.'

"I call Jason often when I have a patient who's feeling defeated and like they have no reason for living because Jason has taken his opportunities as they've come and made the most of his situation.

"For example, with his insurance situation, he wouldn't normally have access to the most sophisticated equipment like he has because A) he was not hurt on the job and B) he is a Medicaid recipient because of his disability, which has very limited funding. But he has found an alternative method to get access to the best prosthetic care because of his affiliation with Touch Bionics and Össur. He's constantly volunteering to try new products or whatever because it not only helps him, it also helps all future prosthesis users as well. And a lot of our patients think that same way, that if they're going through this hell right now, then they might as well use it to help someone else down the road. It's a very giving perspective. And Jason certainly has that quality.

"Jason gives me a lot of credit, but our success here at Arm Dynamics is really due to the fact that I'm allowed to have that much time with each patient to get it right. I'm provided the opportunity to work with one patient at a time instead of 30.

I'll come home and complain to my wife that it was such a busy week because I saw three people this week! My wife is a physician's assistant and she'll just laugh at me because she might see 18 or 20 patients a day.

"But my three patients took up a full 40-hour week because they were all dealing with challenges and we have to figure them out and fix whatever the problem might be.

"In addition to design, the other part of my role is to determine what components are best and most appropriate for the patient. For instance, with Jason, he could not survive day-to-day with just his i-Limb bionic hands. With everything he does, they would break, and then he'd be left without. In his case, it's my job as a prosthetist to look at him and say, 'Look, you go hunting for bears. You don't want your prosthesis to fail when a bear is coming at you.' That's a funny example. But my point is that it's part of my job to find a solution that is going to make the most sense and fit the patient's lifestyle most appropriately. We do have to fit the patient with the correct thing that lets them live their life. Because if they get something they can't use in their everyday life, they're going to leave it in the closet and that's not what anybody wants. It makes our industry look bad."

Again, that's why I stress to amputees how important getting a proper fit really is. I was not successful as an amputee until I got fitted correctly. When it's right, you know. When I put my arms on now, they literally feel like a part of my body. Not like a hunk of plastic and metal and electronics or some foreign object that's strapped to me. They're comfortable and they feel real to me.

From what I've seen and heard from being around all this for a while now, the rejection rate for prostheses is huge. And it's mainly because they're not fitted right. What happens is insurance companies start to not cover prostheses because they've spent a ton of money on prostheses for amputees who never wear them. Insurance doesn't understand why. And actually, the amputee doesn't understand that if you're fitted right, you will wear them and you will be successful. But insurance companies hear the negative experience more often than the positive.

Now I know the difference from personal experience because when I was fitted the first time, it didn't feel as good as my arms do now. But I also was determined back then to be successful and stay active doing things whether they hurt or not. So I did. But now that I'm fitted by Rob, it has been a game changer. I could automatically do more with whatever terminal end I was using at the time. Bionic hands, hooks, it didn't matter. I became so much better at using them just by having a comfortable socket that was fitted right. It makes a huge difference.

And then, when you find the right companies, you stick with them too. Össur and several other companies have done so many things for me to make me more successful with my prostheses. I've been blessed that several companies have wanted to work with me to use their products. So they'll send me stuff to try out and I'll give them my feedback as a user.

BODY-POWERED

"When I say terminal ends, I'm talking about hooks or hands. When I say body-powered, I'm talking about my hooks. They're not electric at all."
~Jason

Body-powered is a very simple setup. You use your body, mainly your shoulders, to move the hooks. They don't work off

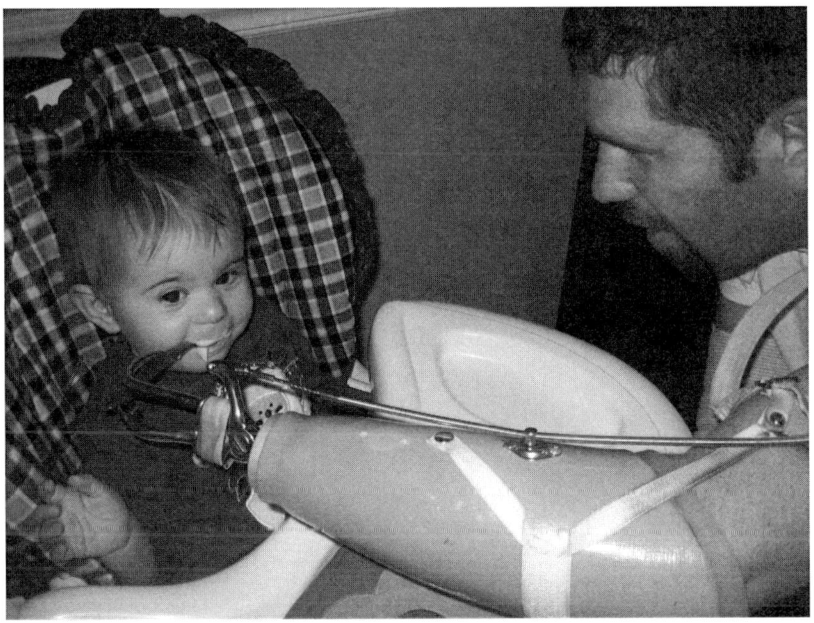

your arm muscles or residual limbs at all. They are cable-powered where a cable runs from the hook all the way up to your opposite shoulder. That same technology has been around since Civil War days.

With my body-powered hooks, my right shoulder controls my left hook. My left shoulder controls my right hook. I have a cable that goes all the way from my hook to the center of my back and straps that go over my shoulders. When I move my right shoulder forward, I'm pulling the cable on my left arm, which opens the hook up. Then when I relax my shoulder, it closes the hook automatically because the hook has rubber bands on it that keep it closed by default. Basically, all I'm doing is using my shoulders to pull a cable. That's why it's called body-powered. It's the same system that's used by a single-arm amputee.

Fillauer is the name of the company that makes my hooks. They're based out of Chattanooga, Tennessee. I've been in their

headquarters. I know the president. Personally, I feel like Fillauer has the best body-powered products out there. I still wear Fillauer hooks today.

The ETD (Electric Terminal Device), which is the myoelectric hook that I wear on my left hand, is also made by Fillauer. That's the one I wore at my TEDx talk.

Having a wrist rotator and wrist flexion unit is also very important for me as a bilateral arm amputee. That's because there are some things I can't do without flexing my wrists. I am talking about everyday things you never realize, like buttoning a shirt. I have to have a wrist flexion unit in order to get to my chest, for example. I couldn't button a shirt or zip a coat without it. My wrist rotator and wrist flexion unit is made by Texas Assistive. It's called a five-function wrist. I tell amputees all the time that if you want the best wrist rotator out there for body-powered, the Texas

Assistive 5 Function Wrist is absolutely the best body-powered I've ever seen, and it's what I wear.

The wrist rotator on my body-powered is basically a button I push with my opposite hook. It's spring-loaded, so when you push that button, it automatically rotates down. To rotate it up you, hold the button and extend your shoulder to pull the wrist rotator up. The wrist flexor is a button too, but you have to push against something to get it to flex down.

MYOELECTRICS

"When I say "myoelectrics," I mean a terminal end that is battery-powered and uses sensors placed on your existing arm muscles on your residual limbs to move it."
~JASON

It's really the socket itself that is myoelectric. When I wear my bionic hand from Össur, that is a myoelectric. When I wear my battery-powered hook from Fillauer, that's also a myoelectric.

Here's how myoelectrics work. They have two electrodes that are sitting inside the socket so they lie right against the skin on your residual limb. Those sensors find certain muscles that trigger them. In my case, I have a little bit of muscle left in my forearm right below my elbow on the top and bottom side of my residual limb. Those sensors are designed to pick up on muscle movements, and when they're triggered, they send a signal that moves my hands.

It's different for every amputee, but for me, when I make the motion that used to raise my wrist in the air, that's what now tells my hand to open. You'll have to put this book down to do this,

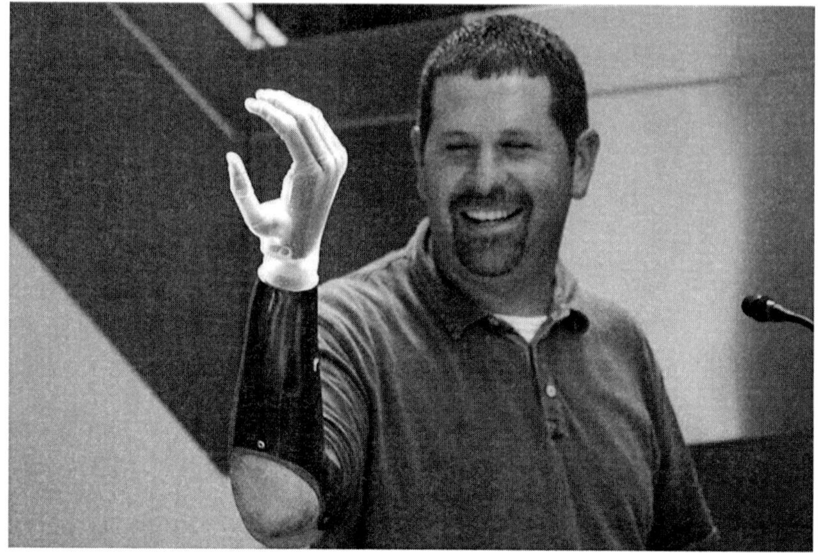

but you can feel what I'm talking about if you hold your right arm straight out in front of you and with your left hand grab just below your right elbow with your left fingers on top of your right forearm and your left thumb underneath your right elbow. (Go ahead, try it!)

Now, with you right arm straight out and your right hand straight out, raise your right hand up toward the sky. Feel that muscle on top flex with your left fingers? That muscle is what tells my hand to open. So, what used to tell my brain to turn my right hand up now means open my right hand. Same muscle. Different motion. I had to retrain my brain in a sense.

Now, with your right arm out and left hand still wrapped around, point your right hand toward the ground without moving your elbow or shoulder. Feel that muscle flex with your left thumb? That's what tells my myoelectric hand to close.

In fact, I could take the sensors off my arm socket and put them right on your skin on those two muscle groups I just told you about and you could fire my hand to open and close. Once those sensors feel those muscles firing, they send that signal. Those sensors are very sensitive. They operate the entire hand. Raise up is open. Lower is close.

But to make the wrist rotator work in my myoelectrics, I have to engage both those muscles at the same time, which is a little tricky. I worked with my therapist to figure that out. But once I learned it, I had no problem.

It's called "co-contract," which means firing both those muscles at the exact same time. When I do that, those two sensors automatically interpret that I want to rotate my wrist around and it will do it as long as I'm still contracting those muscles at the same time. When I relax both muscles, it stops spinning.

That's how I can make my wrist rotate all the way around, which is that little trick I did to begin my TEDx talk.

It took me a little while to get used to it, but those two muscles are what control my hands now. My hands don't open and close by accident or anything. I have to be intentional about it.

Like I said, every amputee is different, but once you figure out how those sensors relate to your muscles, you'll learn to open and close. Actually, my left arm is different than my right arm. On my left arm, my co-contract motion feels to me like giving a quick "thumbs up."

Not to get too complicated in the details here, but I also use those same muscles and sensors to give other commands with my myoelectrics. I can do a double contract or triple contract for other commands too. For example, I could flex "up, up, up" three times in a row to make my hand go into a peace sign or thumbs up or "hang loose" or anything else I have programmed through an app on my phone. There's a video a local radio station made during an in-studio interview that shows you what I'm talking about. If you google "Jason Koger: The Real-Life Bionic Man" you'll find it.

But now, Apple has come out with this thing that uses gyroscopic technology like a cell phone where my bionic hand knows where it is in space at all times. My arm has to be pretty well horizontal with the ground. Then I can hold my hand open, relax just a second, and then move forward, backward, or to the left or right and my hand can sense that movement and go into whatever motion I have it set to do. That gives you four choices.

For example, right now I have mine set to go into a handshake motion when I engage it and move forward slightly because I'd already be moving that direction to shake someone's hand anyway. It's just a natural movement. When I engage it and move backwards, my hand goes into a fist but my thumb goes up a little so I can hold keys in the ignition. When I go left, it goes into a precision pinch, meaning the thumb will line up with my first fingertip almost like an "okay" sign. I can use it when I put a ball cap on or any motion similar to that. Out to my right is tripod, which is where my thumb and first two fingertips will match up perfectly so I could pick something up off the ground or pull something.

I use the term "arm" now very loosely, I guess. Because when I say "my arm," what I actually am describing is my arm socket, the frame that covers what used to be my lower forearm and hides the battery pack, my wrist rotator, my wrist flexor, and then my hand. I mean all those components. It takes several companies to make one arm.

For my right arm, Össur makes my hand and myoelectric wrist rotator and flexor. Arm Dynamics makes my socket.

Then on my left arm, the ETD electric hook is Fillauer. Both my wrist rotators are made by Össur. The arm socket is Arm Dynamics.

My right and left arm are different. I have two Össur i-Limb bionic hands and a full body- powered set. But I have figured out that because I'm a bilateral upper limb amputee, it's easier for me to wear one bionic hand and one ETD or hook because my hook is small enough to slip inside my pocket. A hand is a little bit bigger so it's harder to get inside a pocket. So, when I'm wearing my myoelectrics, I prefer a hook on my left and a hand on my right.

I actually have another video on my YouTube channel that shows what I just explained. Just search for "Jason Koger Puts on Myoelectric Arms" and you can see exactly what I'm explaining.

Nicole Carley, who is the Director of Sales for Upper Limb Prosthesis for Össur, explains:

"Jason has what we call 'dual site control' in our i-Limb hands and that allows him to open and close the hands and enter into different grips suitable for daily living. So what we do for patients is evaluate and find where the strongest flexor and extensor muscles remain. We'll put an electrode on the flexor muscle and one on the extensor muscle.

"That's what Jason explained a while ago.

"In Jason's case, what people don't realize is they are not the same on both sides because of his injury, and surgery, and the way his right arm healed compared to his left arm. The remaining muscle is not identical on his right arm and left arm, so we have to treat them individually.

"So in Jason's case, he's firing different muscles on each side to do bimanual activities like hold a steering wheel, or button a shirt, or cutting food or whatever. So he had to relearn how to control both hands separately and together for bimanual activities, even though he's using different muscles on each arm to control his hands. He's adapted amazingly well.

"So what we do is design these little square sensors called

electrodes that fit inside the socket to detect electromyography, which basically is electrical activity that's generated when a muscle fires. Those electrodes then send that signal to the hand, sort of like an amplifier, that tell the hands to open or close. Those electrodes also sense the amount of force Jason is using with his muscles to control grip strength. That's why it's so important to have a good fit with the residual limb inside the socket so those electrodes fit very snug right up against the skin on the forearm.

"For example, if Jason were picking up a Styrofoam cup of coffee, those i-Limb hands are going to need to slowly close to conform around the cup without crushing it so he can pick it up. So he has to mentally and cognitively control the amount of force on both sides at the same time.

"You and I take for granted the finite muscle control and dexterity we have in our own human hands in simple things like picking up a Styrofoam or paper cup of coffee. But for Jason to be able to accomplish all the daily activities he was able to do before with his natural hands, prior to the amputation, is a miracle. A lot of people give up or get frustrated so what happens is they don't wear their prosthesis.

"Jason was open to trying anything and everything as soon as he could after his accident and he's been able to lead a happy life. As far as I know, he's been able to accomplish anything he's ever dreamed of."

My sister Holly was with me when I got my myoelectrics. She said she would never forget how I put them on and immediately started working my hands. "The prosthetist was shocked," she says. "He slid back in his chair a little bit and was completely surprised. His eyes about popped out of his head and he said he had never seen anyone do that before."

Holly explains how she didn't understand at the time, but what she witnessed while visiting me in the hospital was me preparing for prosthetics:

"I remember back when I saw Jason for the first time after he woke up in the hospital. I thought he was counting to himself. But what he was actually saying was, 'My pointer finger, my middle finger, my ring finger, my pinky and my thumb.'

"I thought there was something wrong with him at first like he had lost his mind. But what he was actually doing was visualizing moving his fingers.

"So that day in the doctor's office when he said that had never happened before, I said, 'Yeah, but you don't know Jason. He's already been practicing this.' It was crazy.

"I don't know if somebody at Vanderbilt told Jason that early on or what. But I remember asking Jenny at the time, 'What is he doing? He keeps doing that over and over again.' But I didn't see him as much in the hospital because I stayed back in the rental condo with the girls so Jenny could be with Jason. But apparently, that's what he was doing. Practicing those muscles. Visualizing his hands moving. Then it all made sense.

"The prosthetist was prepared to teach Jason how to work his muscles and move his hands but as soon as he put them on, Jason started moving his hands right away. It was an amazing moment."

THE RIGHT TOOLS FOR THE DAY

"It takes both body-powered and myoelectrics to do everything I do. I'm fortunate to have both, and I wish every bilateral amputee could have both."

~JASON

People often ask me why I wear body-powered most of the time, and not my fancy, cool-looking bionic hands all the time. They're right, I do. In fact, I'd say I wear body-powered 80% of the time and bionics 20%. At this stage in my life, I'm very active with kids, hunting, and working. I spend a lot of my time at the baseball field, in the woods, mowing, or simply fixing things.

Why would I want to take a hand that might cost up to $100K into the woods, out working in the shop, to a ball field or anywhere else it might get dirt, sweat, or water in the motor? It's not good on them.

If you owned a Lamborghini and a work truck, would you take your Lambo hunting? Why would you do that? On the flip side, would you drive your dirty old work truck on a date when you have a Lamborghini in the garage? You can see what I mean.

The older I get, I think I will to transition more to myoelectrics. When Jenny and I retire, I'll probably wear them all the time. Just like I do when we're on vacation now. But in my day-to-day activities, I usually wear body-powered because I can be rough and tough and not worry about damaging electrical components.

Myoelectrics are way more comfortable than body-powered. But it just depends on what I'm doing that day.

People also ask me how I decide which arms I'm going to wear. Well, it depends on what I'm doing. What is going to help me meet that task for the day? Which arms do I wear today to accomplish everything I need to do today?

Here's an easy way to explain it. If I wake up, and I put on a pair of blue jeans that have grease stains, grass stains, or dirt stains, I'm wearing my body-powered stuff. But if I put on blue jeans that are nice and I don't want to get them dirty, I'm more likely to wear my myoelectrics.

I explain it like building a house. It takes multiple tools.

You cannot build a house with just a screwdriver. You need a hammer, and a screwdriver, and a saw to build a house. It's the same thing with an amputee and prostheses. Prostheses are tools. I need different tools to get through different days. If I'm hunting, that's one set. If I'm working in the yard I need body- powered. If I'm out in public I use my bionic hands. If I'm traveling, it just depends. As an amputee, it takes multiple tools to do what you want to do, especially if you're active.

I feel like things in the world of prosthetics have changed so much in the past fourteen years. Prior to when I got hurt in 2008, the technology was pretty much the same as it had been since Civil War times. Mostly body-powered. But when myoelectric came out, technology started improving quickly and today it's booming. I'm on my fifth-generation bionic hand.

I want to stay up with the times. I want to be at the top of the list for these companies to be sending products to for testing. Össur is based out of Iceland but they have a US branch in California. The engineers are from Scotland. But those engineers know me and they know they can rely on my input. They're brilliant. Sure, they can engineer it and build it but they don't have to wear it. I do. I can wear it for a week or a month and tell them where they need to improve things. What I liked and what I didn't.

They also know that I understand things enough to know how to improve the performance with subtle changes. I can tell them I like this feature or that feature and why. Or I can tell them why I don't like something and make suggestions to improve it. Like, "This is what I wish it would do."

Nicole Carley from Össur speaks again. this time about my role in research and development with the company:

"For us as a manufacturer, I'm excited that Jason is a part of that testing period because we really value his feedback into implementing the design. He's always been a part of our beta and alpha testing and he's a pure joy to work with. All of his feedback has been incorporated into our design so that we can ensure other users around the world can enjoy their i-Limb experience and we thank him for that.

"Jason was the first bilateral upper limb amputee to be fit with bilateral i-Limb bionic hands in the world, and he absolutely rocked it! You would think being fit with two hands at one time and learning two devices at once would take a while to learn. But he adapted so effectively that it was like they became part of his body.

"He has been in every single version of our hand as research and development and technology has evolved over the years. Jason is absolutely the most proficient bilateral arm amputee in the world. It's not only in how he uses the hands, it's really his spirit and his ability to be so willing and so understanding of any advancements in hand technology that we've come out with. It's also his adaptability and eagerness to advance as a prosthetic user.

"It's been a blessing to see him grow as a myoelectric user and to be able to support him in his journey. I couldn't think of any other patient or end user that I'd want to work alongside with as we're developing and advancing this technology to end users around the world. It's just because he wants to help other people that are in the same patient care pathway he is on. He always does his best to ensure they have restored function and can adapt to life with prosthetic hands like he has.

"To see the things Jason's able to do with his hands is extremely motivational and inspiring. When people wake up without hands and think they can no longer live their lives anymore, I always think of Jason and say, 'Yes, you can. You have to meet this guy.'

"Throughout my tenure here, Jason has helped me with many

cases of patients in traumatic situations or accidents. He has truly joined me in helping our customers and patients around the globe feel that sense of hope again and helped them feel like they can do this. That's ultimately because Jason has inspired them by sharing his story and sharing his path to recovery.

"But it's also just how he lives his life. He has this amazing energy that is absolutely contagious. When people get up in the morning and they don't want to get out of bed or might be having a bad day, I want them to think of Jason and picture him popping out of bed, taking care of his family, working on the farm, doing those things in the community, and continuing on. He almost seems superhuman.

"Jason is constantly posting videos on social media of how he cooks dinner or gets dressed or operates machinery on the farm and highlighting how he uses our hands to function and that inspires so many people. By doing that, Jason inspires people around the world every day to not suffer in silence or to not be fearful of exploring prosthesis for function.

"But besides highlighting our technology, I have to say Jason just has the purest heart. I'm a Christian too, and when I look into people's eyes, I can see how pure they are and how thankful they are and I know that he is so thankful for God's grace because he could have died that day in the field, but God had a lot of work left for Jason to do

"We're very fortunate to have Jason as a patient ambassador. We even use Jason on a lot of our literature and advertising. We consider Jason and our other patient ambassadors as part of the Össur family. We can only do so much in design and manufacturing. We lean on our patient ambassadors for peer to peer discussion with other amputees. Empathy is one of the greatest gifts we can have, and Jason is extremely empathetic. He has a gift of expressing what it takes to get through this and he's inspired people around the world. We include him on a lot of these cases in helping patients understand what's in store on the patient care pathway. He shines a very bright light for them on their pathway to recovery.

"Jason is also very humorous and shares his story in such a way that people relate and he's so articulate in getting people to be so thankful to wake up every day and do whatever it takes to get through the day. He definitely helps people reset, be appreciative, and find hope again in the little things in life like being able to cut your food or hold your child's hand and things that are such a gift.

"What Jason went through is extremely traumatic. People have shared with us that losing a limb is like losing a family member. You have to grieve that loss and some people just can't seem to climb out of that loss. But Jason has really helped so many people around the country to have faith, hope, and push forward. He is extremely relatable and simplifies it in such a way that people can relate to him very quickly. You can see how good his heart is by meeting him for just five seconds. You can see it in the twinkle in his eyes. You see that he just wants to do God's work and help people recover and move on.

"I'm so happy for him and I'm blessed to be a part of this industry and part of this company because we work every day to come up with something that's going to be better for people like Jason to get as close as they can to having their human hand back again. I'm blessed and humbled that God brought him into my life and that I have the pleasure to work alongside him as we come up with new technology to change patients' lives."

I have a great example of that research and development testing Nicole was talking about.

About a year ago, Össur came out with something where when I rotated my wrist up, it would rotate up, and if I pointed my wrist down, it would rotate down. I tried it out for them and didn't like it. But I was able to tell them I am way faster with co-contracting. (Which is the simultaneous activation of muscles on opposite sides of a joint.) So I said, "Why don't you make a wrist rotator that can do co-contract but also could sense when an amputee physically rotates their wrist up or down? Because every amputee is different. But if it could do either, then all amputees could use it and they just use whichever feature they want." I also told them maybe they could make an app where you could change the functionality as you got better at using it. It could rotate slower at first but faster as you got better. If you're an early user, you don't want your wrist to rotate too fast at first because you'll overcorrect it. Slow it down at first, but once you get used to it, crank it up and let them speed it up when they're ready.

Now there's an app for a wrist rotator.

ATTITUDE & SELF IMAGE

"Being successful is about attitude. Making that decision. It's 100% thinking about what I want in my life and how I can accomplish it."

~JASON

The last time I was at Vanderbilt, I visited with a teenager who got hurt really bad and I told him everybody looks at this technology with prosthetics now and talks about the opportunities we have now. But the main thing about being successful is not the brand of prosthetic arms you're wearing or the latest technology. It's about attitude.

Self-image is a big deal too. Amputees don't want people staring at them or making a big deal out of it in public or treating us any differently. But I don't care about any of that. I'm happy with who I am. That's a decision too. You have to decide to be happy with what you've got.

The only time self-image ever really bothers me is when I'm at the beach or a public pool. I don't know why, but I feel fine as long as I have something over my stumps. Whether it's body- powered or myoelectrics, it doesn't matter. About the only time I don't have them on is when I'm swimming because I can't get them wet. That's the only time I ever really get self-conscious about my arms, when my stumps are showing.

When I go to theme parks, I use my hooks. If I'm on a water ride I have my shirt off with my body-powered arms on and my straps across my shoulders. That doesn't bother me. I know people are going to look at me either way, if I have my shirt on or off. They see my hooks either way.

But if I'm swimming in a pool, obviously that's just me in the water with my stumps for the whole world to see and that still bothers me a little sometimes.

The first trip to Florida after my accident, I wore my hooks on the beach, no problem. Just playing in the sand or lying on the beach or whatever. But when the kids asked me to go in the ocean with them, I found myself looking around to make sure nobody was looking before I took my arms off and walked down to the water with them. I don't know why.

What I would do is take my arms off, lay them in the chair, and then pick up one of the kids and carry them to the water because I felt like people might notice my stumps less if I was carrying one of my kids. Then once I was in the water I'd swim like normal. But once I got out, I'd be looking for one of the kids to carry again. I think that was more for me than it was for the kids. They didn't need to be carried. I was carrying them because subconsciously that's what made me more comfortable, I guess. I don't know if all amputees feel like that. But I did.

MY GRANDDAD

"We buried my granddad with his prosthetic arm. But if I knew then what I know now, I maybe would have kept it just to have it."
~JASON

For 29 years I knew my grandfather as a single-arm amputee. My whole life, I saw him one time with his arm off. We never knocked when we walked into their house. We just walked in and said "hello" to let them know we were there. Well, that one

time was later in the evening and he must have already taken his arm off. When he heard me that time, he just about ran across the room to put his arm back on. But I did see it out of the corner of my eye.

That was the only time I ever saw him without his arm on, and that was only for a split second. Obviously, he didn't want to be seen without his arm. I never asked him a single question about what it was like for him. It never got brought up.

I've told Jenny now that if something ever happens to me, I'd want to donate my prostheses to someone who can use them because they're so expensive.

I do wonder what kind of relationship he and I might have now if he were still here because we'd have this in common. We could have had some stories, that's for sure.

What were his challenges? What were the challenges for my mom, growing up with him? How did that impact her, and then me? Did some of those memories I have of watching him take care of his family subconsciously influence me more than I realize? My mom has often wondered if by my watching her dad, my granddad, he had some influence on how I handle my own life. Mainly in the way I have always used my situation to teach other amputees, but also other people in general.

My mom recalls a specific moment when that happened: "Jason and I were out somewhere and a child began pointing at Jason's arms. The mother was trying to hush the child and stop his pointing. Jason noticed what was going on and went over to talk to the little boy. He looked down at him and asked if he would like to see his arm. The mom looked embarrassed, but Jason assured her that it was okay. He told her that the child needs to know that things happen, but you can be okay and move on."

My sister Holly talks about how she has seen me interact with curious kids in public too:

"Even when we're out somewhere in public, he's turning that attention into something positive. Kids will be staring and their parents might be trying to shoosh them or distract them or telling them not to stare, but Jason's waving them over so the kids can see his arms up close. He'll be showing them how they work and giving them knuckle bumps or something. He eats that stuff up."

My granddad taught me a lot just by watching him. I don't mind talking to people about my situation, especially kids. My granddad was great at that too.

PUBLIC CONTACT AND WHAT'S NORMAL FOR MY KIDS

"Stares in public don't bother me. I wish that people would be comfortable talking to me about it instead of just staring."
~JASON

I wish when kids said, "Hey Dad, look. That guy's got fake arms," their parents would say, "Yeah, you're right," and approach me or ask me about it rather than cover their mouth up in embarrassment and walk the other way.

I also understand there are amputees out there who may not want that. But for me personally, I wish they would stop and talk so we could talk about it. That way they might leave thinking that's really cool instead of that's weird or scary.

I don't get tired of people asking me questions. I know people are curious. I don't mind talking about it. For most people, I'm the first bilateral amputee they may have ever met. Of course they're curious. Jenny says: "I remember some of Axell's friends were scared of Jason a little bit. Like when they were three or four. But I remember Axell being confused by that and asking what they were scared of, because to Axell, that's just Dad."

None of the girls' friends have ever been scared. But our kids don't know the difference. It's what they grew up with so it's normal to them.

My mom remembers another story:

"Not long after Jason's accident, there was somebody in the house one day and Jason's prostheses were laying on the table for one reason or another. This person looked down and saw Jason's arms laying there, which can be pretty awkward for somebody not used to it, and Billie Grace looked at the guy and she could almost see the question in his mind. She said, 'That's my dad's hands. Pretty cool, huh?'

"She just knows how to read a situation and break the ice. All the kids do. It's just how they've grown up and how they've gotten used to it. And Jason's made it like that, really.

"I remember one year up at the school it was the fall festival and this one kid was dressed like a pirate and had a hook on. So Jason walks up to him and says, 'Can your hook do this?' and started opening and closing his hook. That pirate kid was looking like, 'Oh my goodness!' Like he didn't know what to do or say.

"But that's just Jason being Jason. Making light of it and making people laugh."

My sister Holly talks about some of what was normal for Billie Grace:

"Jason would go through the drive through at some fast-food restaurant with Billie Grace riding along in her car seat. It was just easier for Billie to do certain things. Jason would order and

when they got up to the window Billie would unbuckle her car seat and crawl out. Then she'd dig Jason's wallet out and get the money. She'd crawl over Jason, hand the money to the person in the drive-through window, pick up the sack of food, put it on the floorboard, then buckle herself back in.

"Now imagine that from the drive-through window worker's perspective. But it was Billie Grace's normal routine to help out."

Our kids have always known me the way I am, but Jenny and I were making a lot of adjustments. I always knew we were going to be okay. But things were going even better than I could have imagined back when I was laying there in that hospital bed.

I had no idea then what God had in store for me just around the corner.

I know I haven't talked about my son Axell as much in this book as much as I've mentioned the girls, but that is because he was not born during most of this story. Jenny and I were told after the accident we wouldn't be able to have any more children, but we wanted more. Once again, God's plan for our family was better than what science predicted. Since Axell was born, having a son has been nothing short of amazing. I love teaching him about responsibility, life, and how to be a gentleman. It is crazy how I can see myself in him. His determination, love for others, never quit attitude, faith, and dreams are so great to watch. No doubt my three children have made me the luckiest dad in the world.

CHAPTER 11

CHANGING LANES (MY NEW CAREER)

*"In class they tell you to give a good speech you
have to have an outline and prepare note cards
and organize your points. Well, I didn't have
any of that. My arms were my notecards."*

~JASON

Today, I've got a great setup with Össur and Arm Dynamics. I'm an ambassador for Össur, which means they give me equipment in exchange for being a spokesman for their brand and an example of what amputees can do with Össur.

It's a sweet deal and I'm so fortunate and blessed to have that opportunity.

Any time I can talk to new amputees, I'm happy to do it. Helping amputees learn how to be successful quickly is one of my favorite things to do because I know how much effort it takes to learn how to use prostheses and get back to normal life routines. Sometimes I can show a new amputee how to do something in a few minutes it took me months to figure out.

Becoming an ambassador is another example of God opening doors for me. One after another.

Now, in a way, God uses me to open another door of opportunity for other amputees sometimes just by me showing them what I know. I think that's pretty cool.

The motivational speaking stuff really came as a complete surprise. I would have never dreamed I'd be doing speaking engagements, but I truly believe that's my new calling.

When I say public speaking is the only class I ever failed, I say that jokingly. It wasn't actually an "F." But it was not good, I can tell you that.

It's funny because the whole time I took that class at Murray State I was asking myself why I ever took that class? Why is everybody required to do public speaking? I'm never going to be a public speaker. I'm never going to use this stuff!

But the thing about public speaking is I don't think it's too extremely hard when you have a good story to tell. I don't know how people get up there and speak about something they think or made up. My story comes from my heart because I know it. I lived it. It's not something I made up or created. That's different.

Not long after I got home from my accident, I was asked to speak at an elementary school and a church or two. People wanted to hear my story about overcoming. I said yes and didn't think much about it.

Then a few days before my talk it hit me like, "Oh my gosh, I'm about to get up in front of all these kids and I don't know what to say." I didn't know where to start, or where to go with my story, or what point I was even trying to make.

In the beginning, I overthought it so much. I thought I would come out and hide the fact that I don't have hands at first. I'd wear a long-sleeve shirt and hide my hook or hand in my pocket or behind my back or something like that. In my mind I'd come out all cool and then be like, "Boom! look at this!", like this big reveal.

But that didn't really work out too well. It threw me off and, in my mind, I felt like, "Dude, I've screwed this whole speech up and I haven't even been up here a minute and a half."

I remember being so nervous afterward because I thought the speech was terrible. I told myself I'm not doing this ever again. I'm done. It was a one-time deal and that was it. I remember leaving there and telling Jenny even if I did want to do speeches, they won't ever call me back. It was horrible.

At least that's what I thought at the time. But guess what? The next year they did call me back.

Who would have ever thought?

The next year it was the same thing. They asked me back again. That's when I started thinking that maybe there was something to this public speaking thing. They must have liked it or they wouldn't have asked me to come back.

My sister Holly shares some of her thoughts on my interactions with people:

"The thing that impresses me the most about all of this is seeing how people react to him, especially when he gives a speech somewhere. He's come to talk to our daughter's school and to see the way the kids and teachers respond is really amazing."

I still never have advertised that I do speeches at all. But I've been asked a bunch. It started local, for a long time, but then it got bigger.

Then somebody heard my story somewhere and passed it on somewhere else. It started out right around Owensboro, and then regionally, a couple hours from the house. Since then, I've been all across Kentucky. I've been to Indiana, Colorado, Las Vegas, and all over.

It's amazing how somebody's story can trickle down so many different paths. One person talks to another person and that person tells another and it spreads from there. I got a call this morning from a lady who wants me to talk to a coal mine in-house employee gathering. It's both a safety and inspirational talk. I thought that was interesting.

Last week, I talked to all the linemen at Owensboro Municipal Utilities.

I truly believe that my accident happened for a reason, so I could share my story.

That's why I do public speaking. I feel like this is my path. This is what God wants me to do.

Now I don't get nervous in front of people. I still feel like my presentations could be way better. I guess I'm hard on myself. I do wonder when it gets to the point that I should get an agent and really start advertising and trying to go after being a national speaker. I'm not sure if I'm at that level yet. But everybody who hears me says I should.

This is a good chance to mention and thank Mark McManus, the General President of the United Association of Plumbers, Pipefitters, and Sprinkler Fitters.

Like I mentioned earlier, I was a member of the Local 633 Plumbers and Pipefitters Union before my accident. The union brotherhood has always been supportive of me and continues to be supportive of me, especially now that I give motivational speeches.

Once Mark McManus heard my story through Brotherhood Outdoors (which I'll explain later), he started bringing me in for UA conferences. Those are amazing opportunities and I can't thank Mark enough, not only for bringing me in the first time, but for also bringing me back to bigger events too.

Mark shares his thoughts:

"When I think of Jason, two words come to mind: inspiration

and perseverance. Jason is a wonderful person with an uplifting attitude. His message is that no matter what difficult situations you come against in life, you can persevere. Jason plows along in a positive direction and that is inspiring to his fellow union members and he's a great inspiration to our entire country.

"As General President of the UA, that's an important message to all UA members because we face difficult tasks on the job every single day, and Jason is the epitome of overcoming difficulties and persevering through hard work."

Diane Atkins, OTR, FISPO, is the Assistant Clinical Professor in the Department of Physical Medicine and Rehabilitation at Baylor College of Medicine. She shares about how I speak with her often, and how she feels about my message:

"The power of Jason's message is life-changing to many. Jason has a way of immediately putting someone at ease, drawing them into a conversation, and then hitting it out of the park.

"The time that truly impressed however, was on a stage in Austin, Texas, where Jason had been invited to join me and the President of the American Academy of Hand Surgery, in presenting his keynote speech comparing Jason's multi-articulating prosthetic hand skills to individuals who had been recipients of hand transplantations.

"The audience of over 2,000 hand surgeons was absolutely mesmerized by what Jason could do. This opportunity also enabled us to cross the Atlantic, to present to an international audience in Lyon, France, where Jason shared this experience again to an audience of rehabilitation professionals from all over the world.

"In addition to that, Jason's recovery accomplishments have been shared in part during almost every professional presentation that I have given in the last 10+ years. His amazing skills with his body-powered hooks, ETDs, or electric multi-articulating hands are demonstrated on slides and videos that I share with every audience with whom I interact. These include high school students, OT students, prosthetic and orthotic students, rehabilitation residents, prosthetists, therapists, rehabilitation MDs, orthopedic, plastic, and micro-vascular surgeons. He is an inspiration to all.

"As an occupational therapist who encounters individuals who have recently lost both arms, whenever I have reached out to Jason to share his story, and his abilities to be totally independent, Jason is there. He shares his journey to achieve independence, his heart, and his soul every chance he gets. For young men who suddenly find themselves without hands, Jason can provide the life experience that cannot be explained by anyone except one who has 'walked this walk.' The willingness, time, and heart that Jason shares with others is pure gold."

Hawaii Five-0

"When I got that call, I thought someone was playing a joke on me at first. Why would someone from Hawaii Five-0 *be calling a little ol' country boy from Kentucky."*
~JASON

When I was doing my speaking engagements, my story got out further than just here in Owensboro.

The first time I was on TV was when our local station, which is out of Evansville, Indiana, did a story on me. That got picked up by CNN and they used the same footage from Evansville.

Then it got picked up by the Associated Press and the next

day *Good Day Philadelphia* picked it up. So, I flew up there and did *Good Day Philadelphia.*

Not long after that, I ended up on Dr. Sanjay Gupta's show. That had to do with my prosthetic company. They pitched the story and it got picked up.

The way I heard it, someone from *Hawaii Five-O* googled bilateral amputee with bionic hands and found me that way. Then they reached out to Arm Dynamics to get a hold of me.

I thought it was a joke. But when I found out they were serious, I wasn't about to pass up that opportunity!

The next thing I know I'm packing my bags for a flight to Hawaii to go act for a couple weeks.

I met Dr. Peter Weller in 2013 on the set of *Hawaii Five-O*. He directed the episode I was on, but you may know him as the leading role in *Robocop*, from *Sons of Anarchy*, or lots of other roles he's played over the years. Peter explains how we ended up in that episode together:

"CBS wanted to remake a very famous episode of the original *Hawaii Five-O* called 'Hookman.' I was to direct the episode as well as play the lead antagonist, Hookman himself.

"The production needed someone to 'double,' or stand in for, my missing hands. We needed someone who had the dexterity of firing rifles, driving cars, and loading bullets. Jason was chosen with his 'miracle' hands, and we made friends instantly.

"Jason has returned from near death and an excruciating setback as an amputee to become one of the most positive and motivational human beings whom I know. Jason's finest attribute is his cordiality. There is not a person I have seen him in the presence of that he does not go out of his way in kindness and respect."

Photo courtesy of Jeff Dawn

I got to be around Alex O'Loughlin, one of the stars of *Hawaii Five-O*, as well. We still keep in touch and check in on each other, especially during hunting season. Here's what he had to say about the Hookman episode:

"Peter Weller played the part, but Jason was the star of that episode.

"To be honest, from the moment I met him I was in awe. I couldn't believe how a man who had lost both his hands could be so incredibly dexterous! Nothing was a problem for him and he was more than proud to show off the amazing prostheses he used to anyone who was interested. His generosity of spirit was immediately apparent.

"Upon knowing him for years now the main thing that sticks out to me about Jason is his approach to life. One could assume that after such a loss from such an unfortunate event a person could become dark or jaded. On the contrary, Jason is one of the most enthusiastic, involved, selfless and all-around awesome people I've ever met. He also has insane amounts of energy, which is very infectious when you're in his presence.

"Jason's story is one of fortitude, resilience and sacrifice. When you actually meet the man and hear his story it's impossible not to be inspired. Not just because he lost his hands and still found a way to live his life completely without them, but because you get a glimpse into how extraordinary the human condition really is."

Shooting that episode was a really fun experience. The directors would explain to me what the scene was about, what they needed me to do with my bionics, how they were going to film it, and what it was supposed to look like. Then I would just do it.

Meeting Alex O'Loughlin, Scott Caan, Peter Weller, and all the others was so surreal. I still keep in touch with Alex from

time to time, and Peter and I have become really good friends since then. Which really tripped me out because I remember watching *RoboCop* as a kid and thinking it was the coolest thing.

There's actually a really crazy story about that.

After I did *Hawaii Five-O*, Peter Weller called me and said he wanted to come meet my family and see this community because I told him so much about Owensboro when we were chatting on set.

He made plans to come visit and booked his flight to Nashville and in the meantime Axell was born. Well, I remembered I had this box in the attic with some of my old toys from when I was a kid and I told Jenny I wanted to go up there and get it so Axell could play with them when he got a little older. There were certain Matchbox toys I remembered that were my favorites.

I went up in the attic and pulled that box down. And right when I opened it up I saw a bunch of stuff folded up in there. I pulled that stack out to take a look and the very first thing I saw was an old poster of *RoboCop*, which of course was Peter Weller's big movie back in the '80s.

As soon as I opened that poster I remembered exactly where it came from. It came out of this old Nintendo magazine we subscribed to when we were kids. We used to play Nintendo all the time and they'd have shortcut codes and bonus things in the magazines. That poster was in one of those old magazines and it got stuck in that same box for all those years.

I was holding that poster in my hand and it just struck me. *Oh, my goodness! This dude is about to come to my house!*

I sat up in that attic and thought, why did I save this after all these years? Was I just intrigued by *RoboCop*? Or was it one of those things when God was saying, "Hey man, put this back, because one of these days I will show you that I'm going to open doors for you?"

That movie poster was from the '80s, and it was almost 30 years later when I found it right at the top of the box. The dude is on the way to my house. Unbelievable! That totally blew my mind!

It was one of those moments where I stopped to think, *Wait, how did I get here?* From a pipefitter to an amputee, to hanging out with Robocop on set in Hawaii, and now he's flying here to Owensboro.

That's one thing I'm enjoying about writing this book. It all happened so fast, like a roller coaster the past 14 years, so it's nice to stop and think back on all this.

How did I get to be the first person in the world with bionic hands? How did my story spread from my hometown to across the county to other states and across the country? How did *Hawaii Five-O* find me? How did Apple find me and put me in one of their commercials for the Superbowl?

Photo by Kenny King, Dream Copy Photography

I couldn't have planned all this if I wanted to! Nobody could. It's all God.

When Peter got to my house I told him, "Dude, I've never asked you for an autograph, but I found something you've got to see." I showed him the poster and told him what I just told you.

When I laid that poster out and showed him, he said, "Yeah. I remember that photo shoot. Yes, it was in a magazine."

Jenny is always really cautious about name-dropping and I try to never be like that too, but through different events I've met some famous people. I try not to make a big deal about it because they're all just normal people like us.

But how do you become friends with Robocop? I mean, how does that happen? I still can't get over that.

Another time was when I was talking to Dave Blanton, the vice president of Realtree, at an event in Louisville. We were sitting on a couch talking and Willie Robertson walks over and flops down and starts talking to Dave. The next thing I know Luke

Bryan and Jason Aldean walk over too. So, it's Dave Blanton, Willie Robertson, Jason Aldean, Luke Bryan, and I'm just sitting in the middle of all this! I played it cool but, in my head, I was thinking, *Is this really happening?*

I don't say that to brag. And I don't mention things like that when I speak because I don't want them to come off wrong. I just mention stories like that in this book to make the point that when God opens doors, one opportunity leads to the next and it will just blow your mind.

Here's a perfect example of that.

Doing *Hawaii Five-O* connected me with Össur and Touch Bionics even more because when Touch Bionics saw that episode, they saw what I was really capable of doing with my prostheses. Apparently, someone who worked on *Hawaii Five-O* was filming a commercial for Apple that was supposed to feature how different apps can help people's lives, so when that guy heard how the commercial was to be about how apps can work on prosthetic limbs, he remembered me from *Five-O*.

So, the Apple people called CBS, CBS called *Hawaii Five-O*, and

they connected all the dots that circled back to me just because that guy saw me on the *Five-O* show. That was the connection.

Lynsay Emmrich, who is the Director of Remote Training and Occupational Therapy for Össur, talks about seeing me on *Hawaii Five-O*:

"I was so impressed with how Jason was able to use his i-Limb hands on that *Hawaii Five-O* episode, especially without being able to easily see with the actor, Peter Weller, standing in front of him as he performed complex tasks!

"He was telling us some stories from filming on set in our office soon after he got back home. The experience made everyone laugh as we pictured the interesting scenes he was a part of in the episode. As an occupational therapist, that really interested me since the lack of sensory feedback and extra reliance on visual feedback is frequently described as a challenge with upper limb prosthetic devices.

"I first met Jason when he traveled to the Touch Bionics office in Ohio in 2012. He had been the first person with bilateral amputations fit with the original i-Limb hands several years prior to that time. His experience with the original models provided great input for the team. Jason's mechanical mind allowed him to utilize the hands in amazing ways.

"I also had the great privilege of traveling with Jason to the filming of his appearance as a guest on Dr. Gupta's show, along with his prosthetist, Rob, from Arm Dynamics. I was so impressed with how easily Jason shared the function of the 2013 model of the hand, the i-Limb Ultra Revolution, to Dr. Gupta and how he shared the benefits of the function it provided. Jason was so relaxed on set and just happy to share his story in hopes that it would benefit others.

"After a while it became a bit of a running joke that every

time I would see Jason, he would tell me about another famous individual he had recently met. As we continued to joke about his 'famous encounter' experiences, one time he traveled to the Ohio office again and the story he told us was that time he sat next to a bald eagle on the plane! This eagle was famous for flying over the Super Bowl during the national anthem. There's always a funny story with Jason."

FROM SMALL SCREEN TO BIG SCREEN. SORT OF.

"Being an extra in the movie Free State of Jones *was another random connection."*

~JASON

I got an email that they were looking for amputees for a Matthew McConaughey movie set in the Civil War era and they were only using local people because they didn't have the budget to fly people in.

I was telling Peter about it, and I told him they were looking for amputees. He asked me who the production company was for the movie and I told him. He has a house in Louisiana. Well, because I don't have an agent, Peter basically called the director or producer and told them I had worked on *Five-O*. Peter basically got me that opportunity.

The scene I was in was a very small part. I remember the camera being up close when they were filming, but I went back and watched and I couldn't even pick myself out in the actual movie. It either got cut completely or it was just a fraction of a second on screen.

One thing about the TV and movie industry is you never know what's going to get cut or actually make it on film in the editing process. You still get paid though, so that's cool!

Being on set down in Louisiana was cool. But my part was so small I was only on set for a couple hours one afternoon. I had to grow my hair out and grow a beard and everything.

I did have an agent call me one time from LA, but it didn't go anywhere. He reached out to me and we talked one time. I thought he was bullcrapping me at first, and then at the end he sounded like he thought I was bullcrapping him. He asked me to fill out an acting résumé and I had no idea what that even meant. I asked him what an acting résumé looked like because I'd never seen one.

As soon as I said that, he immediately changed his tone and said something like, "You mean you've been on TV, commercials, and a movie and don't even have an acting résumé?" I explained that I never wanted to be an actor and wasn't pursuing it when all these things just popped up. I told him that something happened to me that's interesting to people and that's where all this came from. When somebody in Hollywood wants a bilateral upper arm amputee with hooks or bionic hands that are the real thing and not set up with a green screen, there just aren't many of us in the world that can do that naturally. I don't think he believed me. He never called back and neither did I.

Sometimes I wonder how big this could be if I actually did try to get an agent and really pursued acting and getting on the national speaking circuit. I feel like I'd fill a niche, especially if somebody needed an amputee for a role. I'm the real thing. A normal, average, working guy.

But honestly, I haven't had time to even look into it. I've stayed busy enough just taking the opportunities God puts right in front of me. So that's where I go.

Sometimes that's a TV studio or a movie set in Louisiana. Sometimes it's speaking at a church or school here in my hometown. But it's always an adventure, and another opportunity to share my faith and the hope I have.

For me, that's what it's all about. I want to share my story with others and hopefully inspire them.

Inky Johnson is a great example of what I hope to be one day. Inky was raised in Atlanta and came from very humble beginnings. He played football from the time he was five years old and was a fullback for Tennessee, where he was expected to be the number one pick in the NFL draft. But in his last game at Tennessee, someone tackled him and injured his left hand to the point he lost all movement in it. Today he's a motivational speaker and he's very good.

I've always looked up to him for the way he uses his injury to motivate others. I actually reached out to him and he responded right back, even though he's a world-renowned speaker, and said one day maybe we could work together somehow.

That's the way I want to be and I hope to be on that same level one day. Just like Inky, I want to use my injury to motivate others and maybe help somebody else. And just like Inky, when I get to that point, I still hope I'll take the time to help the next person who reaches out to me to help them.

Hopefully by now you can see this list of people who have helped me get to a place where I can not only take care of myself, but also still take care of my family. I try to take care of others too.

It took everyone from the first responders to Dr. Guy and the staff at Vanderbilt, to family and friends. Then there is a whole line of others who helped open up new opportunities for me that I never could have dreamed of.

I feel like I owe it to all the people who have helped me over these past 14 years to pay it forward and help somebody else.

CHAPTER 12

RELEARNING OLD THINGS AND TAKING MY LIFE BACK

*"Failure was a good teacher. It's actually a
good thing because it teaches you another way
of doing things. It was just part of the process
of learning to do things a better way."*
~Jason

As you can see from the last couple chapters, things started moving quickly in my recovery. But it didn't start out that way. It was slow those first couple years.

It really came down to being determined to learn how to function on my own. There were so many things I had to learn to do again.

Like how to hold an ink pen, for instance. I know how it feels to hold an ink pen with three fingers. I know the pressure you use in each of those fingers to hold that ink pen and how you use your wrist and fingers to move it to write words. Now how do I do that with hooks? Or metal and plastic fingers that only flex certain ways and a wrist that only bends at certain angles?

I had to relearn to hold an ink pen the way I've done it for almost 30 years. I tried. And failed. And tried it a different way. And failed again. Then tried it again until I sort of had it. Then I got better. Now, it's second nature again. All those little failures were really victories because they taught me what wouldn't work and forced me to try new ways. With every little thing I learned to do again, the process of relearning got easier.

I had to learn how to use a fork, knife, spoon, tools, a remote control, and how to put a belt in my pants. I had to relearn things like holding a steering wheel or using a Weed eater. All these are everyday things we take for granted.

Slowly but surely, I learned how to do everyday things again.

But it was hard. I think it's actually easier to learn things you've never known or done before than it is to relearn something. If it's relearning an old skill in a different way, your brain has to refigure everything. That's really frustrating. I just had to be patient with myself, and I still do.

My dad made an interesting observation about how much I retrained my brain in order to do the things I was accustomed to doing in a whole new way:

"Before his accident, Jason had always been right-handed. Now he does a lot of things left-handed. For instance, he eats with his left hand now. Jason says it's because his left arm got fitted first because his right arm took a little longer. But that means he had to learn most things all over again. It's been amazing to see. Donna and I always say that goes back to his ingenuity. He's always had that kind of inquisitive mind and could figure things out."

In the beginning, I did go to an occupational therapist in Owensboro named Karen Drake who was very supportive and helpful because she pushed me. And that helped tremendously too. But she was learning right there with me. She would give me ideas of how to try things. Then I would try them. And we'd talk about it and try it again. Together we got it done. It's a slow process.

Lynsay Emmrich shares her experience with me:

"The most impressive thing about Jason to me is how he accomplishes everyday tasks. These are the things we all take for granted such as opening a bottle of soda, holding our kid's hand while crossing the street, or cutting up a good steak. Not only has Jason mastered using his prostheses to accomplish these tasks, but he has found meaning and purpose in helping others to be successful as well. He loves helping others figure out how to do these everyday activities and shares videos and advice.

"Jason has taught me so many things as a therapist that I have been able to share with others learning to use prostheses. Everyday things like how to use the bathroom or shower without arms. While it may not have been a path he would have chosen for himself, his life post-amputation has had a positive influence on so many individuals.

"I'll share one last story. In many of our travels together for conferences showing how the i-Limb hands are used, I've had the opportunity to enjoy meals and social activities with Jason. Once at a bar, they had the giant Jenga set up. We played in teams with four people and altogether we had five intact hands between us.

"Jason kicked all our butts, with a drink in his electric hand and using his electric hook to pull out the blocks!

"It makes my heart happy that Jason has not only accepted his limb loss but sees it as an opportunity to help other individuals that have had similar experiences."

It's funny the things you learn the hard way. I know now where the strongest part of an aluminum can is. If you grab a can of Diet Coke too hard in the middle of the can with a set of hooks, it all comes squirting out the top. I know I have to handle that can a certain way with a certain amount of pressure, not too hard to crush it, but not too lightly so it slips out of my hand again.

You probably never even think about that. You just wrap your fingers around it and go. But I know I have to aim my hooks right under the top of the rim where the metal is strongest to open it. Then once it's opened, I can grab it a little lower so I can tip it back to drink. Then I use a little less pressure once it's opened. I have to take that first drink a little slower because it's all the way full or else I'll spill it on the way up to my mouth.

I had to relearn all that. It's not like there's a "how to drink a Coke with no arms" class out there. Now it's second nature to me again.

Whenever I reach for a drink people ask me all the time if they can open it for me. But then when I say, "Naw, I've got it" and open it with no problem, they are surprised and can't believe it. They think it's the coolest thing. I'm just thinking that I'm thirsty.

The same thing happens when I'm in a restaurant cutting a steak or eating a salad. I don't need people to cut my food for me, but people constantly offer to help. I just have to hold my arms a certain way to get the right angle to cut things with a knife. I don't even think about it anymore. But I bet other people think it looks awkward. My elbow sticks straight out instead of down at my side like yours does when you cut a steak.

People also freak out when I answer their texts immediately after they send them to me. I know they are thinking, "Wait, how does a guy with no fingers text?"

Well, the trick is that I have an Android phone and I can text easily with my hooks. That's because Androids are touch-sensitive and not skin-sensitive like Apple products. I can text by dragging my hook tip and connecting the letters to make words quickly. I'd bet I can text faster with my hooks on an Android than you can with two thumbs on your iPhone.

But if I want to use my iPad, I have to throw my arms off and use my nubs because Apple screens are skin-sensitive. It's like it would be for you if you were working your iPad with the tips of your elbows. Clumsy at first. But you could learn.

Using my iPad or sending emails are about the only times I don't have my prostheses on now. But it wasn't like that the first couple years after my accident, for sure.

I can get in and out of my arms pretty quickly now, especially with my body-powered harness. I keep them loose enough so that I can slip my arms off pretty easily in just a few seconds. Then it takes maybe 30 seconds to put them back on. That took me a while to learn. Just like anything, it's practice.

My mom recalled that Billie Grace was my hands for a while. She would go before me and do things for me. It got to the point where she knew what I needed before I even said anything. For instance, one time I dropped my keys in between the seats and Billie automatically said, "That's okay! I'll get them."

Mom goes on to talk more about Billie Grace during those days:

"One time, when Billie Grace was really little, I was there and heard Jason tell her, 'Billie, go back the truck out the driveway and up to the barn.' Shocked, I said, 'Jason, there's deep ditches between there. She can't do that.'

"He looked at me and said, 'Mom, she can do it.' And he was right. She got in the truck and did it, no problem. If he told her that she could do it, then she believed she could. She could barely see over the steering wheel, but she backed that thing right up and out of there.

"She would drive him around on the farm, and that's how she learned. Not on the roads, of course. It's not something you would normally see a child do, but it was normal in their lives."

MY FAMILY HELPS AND CHALLENGES ME

"Sometimes I had to push Jason a little bit in some ways. But I knew I could because I believed in him and I could see how hard he was trying."

~Jenny

In the beginning, I did go to an occupational therapist who was very supportive and helpful because she pushed me.

I tell everybody I can do everything I used to do except for three things: dirty diapers, cooking, and cleaning. Or anything else I decide I just don't want to do anymore. People usually laugh at that joke. Jenny just rolls her eyes or slugs me in the shoulder.

Jenny pushed me to do a lot of things on my own. We laugh now about one story she tells.

"With three kids, plus Jason, I got tired of putting four pairs of socks on every morning after I had put my own on. I just thought he needs to figure this out on his own. I knew he could do it.

"One day we had somewhere to be and I just walked across the street for a minute so he wouldn't have a choice. It sounds mean saying it out loud, but I knew he could do it.

"And you know what? I came back and he had his socks on.

"That doesn't mean that I still don't put his pants on every morning, put his belt on, put on his deodorant for him, and sometimes, yes, put his socks on for him. I do. But he can do it all himself. It just takes him a lot longer.

"Like at three o'clock in the morning when he wakes up to go hunting, he does it all himself because my head is still on the pillow. I joke and tell him I don't love him that much to get up when he goes hunting! I mean, come on!

"But yes, he learned to do everything himself. We just do things for him sometimes now out of convenience but not necessity anymore."

My dad challenged me on some things too. He had an old piece of machinery at his shop that wasn't working right. Right after I got my prostheses, he brought it over to me to tinker with it. He says:

"Whether he fixed it or not, that wasn't the point. It just gave him something to do to get his mind off things, so that way he could go down to the garage and put his mind to that.

"But I think he enjoyed taking it apart and putting it back together. He tries anything.

"I figured he would call me when he was done to come get it. But sure enough, he loaded it by himself. I think he lifts too many things himself and does too much without asking for help, actually."

I worked on that thing for weeks. I think it was a part of a boiler. It was basically a motor on a stand with some tanks and gauges on it. I took it apart and put it back together just to get experience using different tools again. That was one way I got to tinker and get better at using a wrench and a screwdriver again. It was good practice.

My dad told me to let him know when I was done messing with it and he would help me load it back up and haul it off again. I remember thinking that I wanted to load it up by myself without calling Dad. The challenge was in how I was going to load this 750-pound piece of metal on the back of my pickup with fake arms.

I took it all apart, then strapped each piece to an engine stand. Jacked it up off the ground. Backed the truck under it. Then let it back down. Slowly. One piece at a time. Then I hauled it all off to the scrapyard. All by myself.

I did that for no reason other than to say I did it myself. Just to do it.

That's sort of how it was with my recovery process. I knew it was going to be baby steps. But I could make forward progress. There was trial and error and learning as I went.

It all goes back to attitude. I had so many people helping me in so many ways and believing in me that it was easy to believe in myself.

Just like that hunting story with my buddy Sam I told you about. I could have given up hope to ever get back in the woods again. But Sam wouldn't have that. He gave me hope and took me out there and showed me how we were going to do it. We figured it out.

So that's how I got my life back. I found out I could still hunt; we just had to do it a different way.

I could still work a wrench and a screwdriver; I just had to be patient with myself.

I could still be a good husband to Jenny, who always stood by me, and a good dad to my three kids, which was always my greatest goal.

My brother-in-law Toby Alexander has some thoughts about how remaining positive and determined had an impact on my putting my life back together. Toby says:

"If anyone was ever going to turn lemons into lemonade it's Jason. But I'd say he's even exceeded our expectations. For him, it was deciding that not only was he going to turn his situation around, but he was also going to use it for good and become a motivational speaker and be a source of inspiration for so many people. As well as for his own personal gain by putting himself out there in the acting world. He's had some pretty cool experiences that have come from his personality and willingness to fight and keep going.

"But it all points back to his drive and determination. There are different ways to go when something like that happens. You can dive into the bottle. Or end up in a deep, dark depression. As many times as we've been around him in the past 14 years since his accident, I can count on less than one hand the number of times he's ever complained or been down on himself and that's a testament to the faith and the support system that Mike and Donna have built for Holly and Jason at a young age. You never know how you'll react until something like that happens but I can't imagine anybody having a more positive outlook than he has or being more willing to make the most of a bad situation."

I think I understand more now that life is not about material things. Happiness is not about what we own or being famous or many of those things that most of us think will bring happiness.

Faith. Family. Community. Whom you surround yourself with. That's what's important.

That's true for everybody, no matter what circumstances we've had to face in life. We all have our struggles. But when we're going through our tough times, no matter what they are, can we focus on what really matters?

I think spreading that message is my new purpose in life and my deeper calling.

Looking back now, I can say that before my accident I went to work every day and enjoyed it. But I didn't go to work every day thinking, "Heck yeah, man! I can't wait till this day starts." I enjoyed what I did and I liked working for the family business. They say I was pretty good at it. I know I was helping our clients and providing for my family and I know there's honor in that.

But now, I feel like, "This is it! This is what I'm supposed to be doing!"

I look forward to every day, whether I'm talking with a new amputee somewhere, or sharing my story in a speech, or visiting a new patient in the same burn unit I lay in for almost two weeks. I know I'm helping someone.

I'm not excited that I lost my hands and I'm not bragging about the people I get to meet. I do enjoy that part of it. But what I realize now is that because of this amputation I've found my deeper calling in life.

I get to really help other people and I love that! I did before, in a way. It's just in a much different way now.

I think I would still be working in my father's business if I'd never gotten hurt and I would still be happy now, because I was happy then. But my purpose in life now is different. It feels more like my true calling because it feels like a greater purpose to me.

Not to say that is why it happened, or that losing my arms was worth it. I'm not really trying to compare the before and after. I'm just saying that I really like feeling like I have a purpose for my life. This is what God wants me to do with my circumstances.

But that's because I believe God calls all of us through our circumstances.

Even when we can't make sense of them.

It took me a long time to see that, but I totally believe it today more than I ever have.

Having that realization is what motivated me to do whatever I could and to use every opportunity to help other people through my circumstances.

That is when I really started giving back to others the way so many others had helped me—sharing my story anytime anyone asked, raising money for others in my community, and volunteering my time to help other amputees.

When God opens a door, I'll run right through it!

THE MISSION TO HELP OTHER AMPUTEES

"The benefit to patients by hearing from Jason is tremendous. We can reassure them as much as we can. But to hear it from someone who's actually lived it and been in these rooms once themselves . . . is invaluable to patients because they can't get that information from us."

~MEGAN BERGFELD

I enjoy talking to other amputees, and I can usually show them a thing or two that I've picked up along the way that can help them out.

A couple months ago I got a phone call about a bilateral upper limb amputee similar to my situation who was having a hard time using his prostheses. This guy spoke Spanish, so they brought in a translator and Facetimed me from the occupational therapist's office so we could all see each other.

We spent about 45 minutes on Facetime just talking and I was showing him how I do some things. He had a whole new set of challenges. But I knew I could share my experience to help him out with some of the everyday basics.

When I started talking to him, I could tell right off the bat that he didn't have a proper fit yet. One of the first things I was able to show him was how I get in and out of my harness with my body-powered prostheses without needing anyone's help. I broke it down step-by-step. Slipping out of them is a little bit easier than putting them on. Putting them back on smoothly takes some practice, but I was able to show him that slowly, step-by-step.

Next, I showed him some dressing tricks like looping your belt through your jeans before you put them on. Trying to do this after you have your jeans on is a real pain for people with prostheses. Another simple tip is to wear slip-on shoes or the kind with Velcro straps instead of shoelaces.

Then we had a whole lesson on getting ready in the morning. Showering is a whole new challenge for a new amputee. I showed him an oversized loofah with a long string that I use. There is a company that makes them for people with mobility issues. I can handle it with my residuals and it makes showering a whole lot easier for me.

To wash my hair, I use a massage brush that I zip-tied to a suction cup on the shower wall. I hung it up about forehead height. I pour shampoo right in my hair and rub my head up against the massage brush. That setup works great.

When it comes to bathroom business, the use of the paperwork takes a little practice, but it's doable. Plus, there are gadgets available to help with that too.

An electric toothbrush is easier to hold on to with residuals than a regular toothbrush. So, that's another thing I showed him. Anybody can open a tube of toothpaste with their mouth if they had to. I learned how to twist it off. But a flip cap is much easier than a twist-off. I can grab the tube with my residuals and squeeze the paste on the toothbrush. At this point the entire process doesn't really take me any longer than anybody else.

I might look like a T-Rex, but who cares.

More than anything, just hearing from somebody who's in the same boat as you and has "been there, done that" is great motivation and encouragement from one amputee to another.

I just try to be real with them, try to show them it's not that big of a deal. Anything is possible. A lot of times it comes down to sharing stories with each other. The more questions they ask, the more I can help them.

Almost every time they walk away, they are in much better spirits than they were when we started. I love that.

People are impacted in the same way by the support in the burn unit at Vanderbilt too.

Remember, I was lying in the burn unit and Andy came and talked to me as a peer supporter. The moment was huge for me because his story really impacted me.

I still think about it a lot because it helped me most to reconsider how to deal with what happened to me. I remember thinking if he can make it, I can make it. I have it easy compared to Andy. I lost my hands. He lost his family. He had to bury his wife and kids.

There's no one person out there whose story is the worst possible. There's always somebody who is worse off, and somebody better off too.

Andy's story helps me remember that things could be worse, and tomorrow should never be taken for granted.

If I can help somebody else the way Andy helped me, that's definitely worth the two-hour drive to Vanderbilt.

Megan Bergfeld, who is a Peer Support and Volunteer Coordinator in the Burn Unit at Vanderbilt, talks about the value of peer support visits to the patients in the burn unit:

"Jason is one of our peer supporters for patients in the burn unit and who was just trained through the Phoenix Society SOAR program this past year. But he was with the trauma survivors network way before that.

"SOAR is a newer program. It stands for Survivors Offering

Assistance in Recovery and is run through the Phoenix Society, the national burn survivor's organization.

"Jason works primarily with burn injury patients that result in amputations. I wasn't here when Jason was here as a patient, but I've met him several times because he comes here pretty often. Just this past December, for example, Jason just showed up one day completely unannounced to just walk through and check on things. It actually worked out perfectly because we were about to call him anyway. Luckily, he just showed up on his own.

"It's such an important role. Hearing from a survivor like Jason is a tremendous benefit to patients. As staff, we can do our best to reassure them, but to hear from someone who's actually lived it is much more convincing. Their experience is invaluable to patients because they can't get that firsthand information from us.

"It's helpful for them to have the ability to ask questions they know we don't know the answers to. Questions like how long will this hurt? How long does it take for my skin to stop feeling itchy? We can't answer those questions the way a survivor can. That firsthand knowledge is important.

"It's also extremely helpful for our patients to see that years later you can be a perfectly functional, happy person. Like Jason. It's just life's a little different for them now."

Dr. Guy shared with me that he was not supportive of me coming to talk with other patients at first. He says:

"In the beginning I was afraid he was being used because I thought it was way too soon. I thought he needed to be focusing on himself. I thought he should be focusing inward, not outward.

"But he did fine with all that. He did great. I was wrong. Maybe I was just being protective of him a little.

"It took me a while to come around. But it was obviously a

good thing. Jason would come around the clinic and everyone would be happy he was coming. Jason was also happy.

"When he was on the clinic schedule, he was like a ray of sunshine. He wasn't asking me for pain medication or OxyContin the way some former patients do. Those suspicions are always there. But with Jason, they never came up.

"There were no red flags. Just a bunch of smiles."

Photo by Danny Beeler, Heart of the City Design

Photo by Kenny King, Dream Copy Photography

CHAPTER 13

HANDING BACK AND OTHER EVENTS

"It's important to me to give back to my hometown community because they gave so much to us when I got hurt. I don't mean just financially. People supported my family in so many different ways it was amazing."
~JASON

Another way I try to give back is through a foundation and fundraising event called "Handing Back." It's basically my way of giving back to my community after they rallied around me and my family so generously after my accident.

A fundraiser was put on by some of our friends before Handing Back came about. That money was used to pay some of my medical bills. That was the inspiration for what became the Handing Back Foundation. The idea was to have a big fund-raising event here in Owensboro to raise money for grants to be given back to the community.

That first Handing Back event was put on not long after I got back from *Hawaii Five-O*. Peter Weller wanted to come to Owensboro to meet the community and the people who helped me. We coordinated that event to coincide with his arrival. Of course, Peter being here was a big draw for attendance and helped in a huge way with its success.

We charged for admittance and raised $18,000 at that first

Photo by Kenny King, Dream Copy Photography

event. We gave that money to seven different charities. When Peter returned for the second event, we raised $21,000, which we gave to elementary schools to fill their Christmas wish lists. That Christmas Wish program helps needy families during the holidays. Now we have a board that decides where the money gets distributed.

We also invited Dr. Guy to come up for that first fundraiser because I wanted to present him with a plaque in appreciation for all he's done for me and my family. That was a special moment for me. Dr. Guy talks about arriving at that fundraiser:

"Jason invited me to come up for a fundraiser up in Owensboro and I drove up with my daughter to attend the event. This was only a few months after Jason's accident so my daughter was only eight years old at the time.

"Jason met us in the parking lot, so I introduced my daughter to Jason and told her, 'This is the guy I was telling you about.'

Jason walked up to us and stretched out both arms like he was really excited to see her. But what he said was, 'Look, your daddy did this to me!'

"He was totally kidding and smiling ear to ear when he said it, but she looked at his arms and then looked up at me and was horrified!

"I could have killed him!

"The whole family is so funny like that. It was a fun night."

Peter Weller was there on that first night and had a huge impact on the success of Handing Back and in helping to get the concept started. But there are other people who have shown up too.

I have met many friends through the shows, hunting trips, and other events I've been to since I started traveling to share my story.

Because of all those little connections, I was able to call on some of those buddies to help me out with the Handing Back events here in Owensboro. In the first couple Handing Back events we've had Peter Weller, Chad Warrix from the band Halfway to Hazard, and several singer/songwriters from Nashville including Buddy Owens, Billy Dawson, Galen Griffin, and Ray Stephenson, who's written songs for Johnny Cash and Willie Nelson. We also had a lot of local artists and musicians who performed as well, including speed painter Aaron Kizer, Jaclyn Graves, Elliott Sublett, Josh Merritt, and the band Insulated. My buddy Reggie Showers also attended, who is a bilateral leg amputee but still became a two-time NHRA drag bike world champion even though he was told as a kid he would never be able to race.

The crowds are amazing and the nights are always fun. Good food, good music. A few little inspirational speakers. We keep it light and fun.

We also have silent and live auctions to raise money for charity. My dad talks about the award I presented to Dr. Guy at that first fundraiser, and a fun twist that happened at the auction at that event:

"That night, we wanted to give Dr. Guy and his nursing staff an award to thank them for all that they had done.

"So Jason was up on stage and he started talking about Dr. Guy. At one point Jason started getting emotional and he paused a little bit to get his emotions under control. I could tell he wanted to cry inside, not outside.

"I walked over to him and said, 'Jason, go ahead. It's okay. You've got to finish your speech. Just keep going.' Jason swallowed hard, and just kept going. He got through it and gave Dr. Guy his award.

"Dr. Guy was so nice and the crowd really clapped for him that night when Jason was thanking him on stage.

"But the funny thing was that at one part of the night there was an auction. They started bids on this pair of boots that I really liked so I started bidding on it. Well, there was one other guy in the crowd that kept bidding on it too. For a while it was just me and him, running up the bids on this pair of boots.

"This other bidder finally dropped out and I ended up winning it. Then toward the end of the night I was talking to Dr. Guy and he told me that he was really hoping to get that pair of cowboy boots but some other guy kept running it up and he dropped out.

"So I said, 'You're kidding me! I was bidding on them. And I got 'em!' We both laughed at how funny that was. But then I said, 'Here you go. You can have them.' We got a big kick out of the two of us bidding against each other from across the room. Those boots didn't fit me anyway. They weren't my size. I was happy for him to have them.

"It was nice to have some laughs in some happier times like that after going through those hard times together in the hospital."

Once we can gather in large crowds again (after COVID), we'll start planning our next Handing Back event. I like to have them every couple of years so I can invite new people whom I've met.

That's sort of how it works with my travel schedule. I'll get invited to events through some connection or another. Then I'll meet people at that event and I might become friends with some of them. Then I can invite some of those friends to my charity event. The people involved in charity events like that like to help each other's projects. It's really cool to be a part of it

I have attended too many charity events to count. I know that the favor will be returned going forward and my friends will attend a Handing Back event. But I am going to mention a few events and names to put them on the spot. I am kidding a little, but then again, I'm not.

In the middle of writing this book, for example. I was invited by Tim "TK" Klund to play in a charity softball event down in Texas called the Red River Celebrity Softball classic. It usually has actors, professional athletes. Of course, the 2020 event got canceled because of COVID-19, but I got to go to the 2021 event. Here is what Tim said about that event.

"One Saturday morning in 2020, I was with my wife, she was inside at her hair appointment and while I was waiting, I was surfing Facebook and came across this inspirational video of Jason Koger.

"At first, I thought he may have been in the military, so I tuned in. After watching the video I was so inspired I tracked him down through Facebook and sent him a message that I would love for him to come play in my Celebrity Softball Classic event in Arlington, Texas.

"I left my cell phone number in the message and a few minutes later he called and we were having an amazing conversation! Growing up in southeast Missouri myself, Jason and I hit it off, being country boys from the same area. We spoke for over an hour and I sent him all the information on the 2020 game. A short time later he replied that he was 'in' for the celebrity game.

"Not long after that call, the world was locked down due to COVID-19, so the 2020 game got canceled but we did have the game in 2021 at Globe Life Field (where the Texas Rangers play) and Jason was able to come out and join in the fun. Being the first game for this series, I wasn't sure if there would be a second game, so I made sure most everyone I knew got to come and play. With that said, we had two games: one veteran coed game and a celebrity coed game after that. I had over 60 players per team, 120 players per game, so almost 250 celebrities and veteran heroes were in attendance for the Celebrity Weekend. Now, we had some AMAZING celebrities and American heroes having fun and the feedback I received from almost all my attendees is how much they all loved Jason!

"Everyone who came in contact with him or got to spend a little time together with him during the weekend was blown away by his humbleness and genuine personality! I have worked with professional athletes and celebrities for 20 years and I can tell you that Jason is absolutely one of my favorite individuals to hang with.

"Also, one of the coolest things from the game and to further show how much everyone loves Jason, his prosthetic team made him personal prosthetics for the game. They made him two prosthetic devices, one with a glove for playing in the field and another prosthetic to bat with. Both of those prosthetic hands paid off, because he caught a pop fly in right field and threw it to the second baseman without issue. He also got a hit when he came up to bat.

"Truly inspirational!

"The best thing for me personally was every time I saw Jason, he had the BIGGEST smile on his face! Whether it was Friday night at the VIP meet and greet party, Saturday hanging out with everyone at the hotel pool, or Saturday night at the game, he was having the BEST time!

"To me . . . that was the BEST feeling of the weekend!"

I have met many other cool people over the years. The first musician I met was Chad Warrix from the country band Halfway to Hazard. He's also written several songs for Nashville stars. He invited me to a four-wheeler charity ride over in eastern Kentucky where he's from. I showed up and MMA fighter Rich Franklin was there. Tim McGraw couldn't make it that year, but he came in his helicopter the year before and sang a few songs. They had an all-access pass with my name on it when I got there. It was really cool.

From there I met other people at other events. One time I was invited to do a pheasant hunt with Operation Cherrybend, which is a charity to help wounded veterans. Every year they do a concert and a hunt to benefit veterans. I wasn't really thrilled about going because I told them I'm not a veteran and I never served. But they said it didn't matter; they wanted me to be an inspiration to other amputees.

I decided to do it and they sent us out on a tour bus from Nashville to the event. There were several singer-songwriters from Nashville involved, including Jared Ashley, who is also a US Navy veteran and the founder of Operation Cherrybend. He has become a great friend and has a lot to say about my visits with the veterans and the Cherrybend event.

"When I was first introduced to Jason, I knew he was an outdoorsman. I also knew he had lost some limbs and had an inspirational story. But I wasn't really keen on the idea of having Jason involved in events with combat veterans who had maybe stepped on an IED and lost limbs. But once I met Jason and was able to witness his interactions with people, I realized that just because he never served in the military doesn't mean his injuries are more or less impactful than someone who suffered loss during deployment.

"Just seeing Jason firsthand around all these veterans and how he lifts them up is amazing to see. What he teaches them is there's nothing you can't do! This guy is missing both hands and living a normal life, which is very inspirational for someone who is missing one leg, or one arm, or some fingers.

"What he's done with me in the veteran community is almost better than what a veteran can do. Veterans are known to be tough and trained to persevere, then you meet a guy like Jason Koger who had never been to boot camp or had any official survival training. What he had is his faith in God. It's his faith that pushed him to survive. There's no amount of training that can force you to accept your injuries.

"I remember Jason was a little uncomfortable coming at first because he's not a veteran. But I told him, 'You're here to inspire! You're more important than these celebrities I invited because you're one of them. They're not in the military anymore, either. They're just like you. They're out here hunting, fishing, climbing trees in deer stands, and loading up crossbows. You're all in the same boat now.'

"It's hard to put into words what Jason does for the veteran community. The way he takes care of himself and provides for his family is an inspiration. Honestly, Jason probably does every-thing better now because he's so driven.

"Believe it or not, it's not easy to get the right veterans for Operation Cherrybend. They need to be outdoorsy, into hunting, able to adapt, and have the right personality. My buddy Ron Champion told me about this guy Jason from Kentucky that is a double-arm amputee and is a really good guy, but the only thing is he's not a veteran. At first, I said no way. But Ron said, 'I understand. But take him up there one time and you'll see.'

"I didn't meet Jason until that event. But now, I invite him everywhere. Everybody loves him. He actually doesn't realize how much of an inspiration he is to people. He loves to tell his story, and it's easy for him. He tells it like it's no big deal, but to everybody else it's mind-blowing.

"Veterans can be down on themselves. Sometimes VAs will overmedicate. A lot of times veterans will turn to alcohol or drugs to self-medicate. They may get very emotional, moody, and not be pleasant to be around. Then we throw Jason into the mix and here comes this guy missing both hands but is genuinely happy and full of life and is fun to be around. It's really cool to watch.

"There's so much we can learn from Jason. And not just amputees, but even us everyday folks.

"By inspiring others through his appearances at so many different events, he has probably saved more people's lives than he will ever know.

"He makes an impact everywhere he goes and in everything he does. Jason is just an average, normal guy. It's a weird thing to say but losing his arms has given Jason so many opportunities that he would never have gotten before. But the reason he gets these opportunities is because he gives so much. I bring Jason in to do these events because I know he will influence people's lives from just being around him.

"That's what makes him great. He is a normal dude that has done some extraordinary things.

"How many people was Jason impacting before his accident? How many people is he impacting now? Who knows, maybe the whole reason he was shocked by that power line was so he could change the world.

"I can tell you that when you're around him, you feel that. He doesn't look at it as an accident. He looks at his story as his mission."

I met other singer songwriters through Operation Cherrybend too. People like Lewis Brice, who is country star Lee Brice's brother, Buddy Owens, Ray Stephenson, and singer Mark Wills. The last time Chris Jansen was in St. Louis I was able to go backstage and meet him because my buddy Bruce Swearingen called Chris's road manager and got me tickets. Chris is a big hunter too and he says he remembered seeing a picture of a deer that I killed.

Bruce is how I met Jason Aldean too. I'm good friends with LoCash. I got to hang out with them in St. Louis and they've played Owensboro several times.

Jared Ashley also introduced me to Ted DeBiase Jr. at a Cherrybend event. Ted is an actor, former WWE champion, and a businessman. He too has become a friend and talks about that friendship and our mutual love for the veteran's charity events.

"Jason Koger is one of my favorite people in the entire world. He's the most personable, most sincere, most genuine, most humble person I've ever met in my life.

"I was a wrestler in the WWE for a while and had the opportunity to be a spokesperson for the Army National Guard, which was great because I always considered myself a patriot and admirer of our nation's heroes. Cherrybend has become one of my favorite events. It honors veterans that have been disabled or suffer from invisible wounds like PTSD. But much like Jason, their disabilities are not actually disabilities at all. They're just new challenges to overcome.

"What I've noticed though is that a lot of times soldiers who are newly injured don't have that strong community they're used to in the service once they get back home. So they isolate themselves. They see themselves as used up.

"Just imagine being one of the baddest dudes on the planet, maybe a trained operator or special forces. But then all of a sudden you step on an IED and you lose both your legs. Thankfully, your brother saved you and the next thing you know, you've woken up at Walter Reed (military clinic). That's a rough transition. One day you were fighting bad guys and the next second you've got a whole new life.

"In that situation, they not only lost the use of their legs or arms; on top of that, they're suffering from what they've seen in war and those are some gruesome things. Some guys' wives can't handle it and they lose a lot personally as well. So, they isolate themselves. That's partly why 22 service members a day commit suicide.

"A guy like Jason inspires them. When those wounded warriors see him and his spirit of being such a joyful person, it just lifts their spirits. Which is a natural result of being around Jason. After suffering such a horrendous, traumatic event, when you get to hear his story and see the way he responded, it's so inspiring.

"We all have choices. We make 84,000 choices every single day and that's what formulates our life. I believe how we choose to respond to the traumatic, uncontrollable events in our life are some of the most defining moments of our life, because it's basically a crossroads. You can live the life of a victim and be mad, angry, and bitter. Or you can take what God's given you and look at it as an opportunity. And as you've been reading, that's what Jason did.

"The Bible says to take joy in trials of many kinds for that develops perseverance, and perseverance must run its course so that you're not lacking in anything, so that you are complete. That is what I think about when I think about Jason Koger. (That scripture is in the book of James 1, chapter 1, verses 3-4 if you want to look it up.)

"I think about these wounded warriors who don't have a mentor at home or lost their identity as a hero and now they can't find it. Then you have a guy like Jason—and I've seen him do this over and over—he gives them so much more insight, perspective, and support than what they're given when they come home, especially when they've been dismantled and mentally destroyed.

"It's not only Jason's story, it's also his presence. It's seeing the life he's still able to live after his physical wounds have healed. He has given them so much hope that life doesn't have to end, and that you can use this tragic event that has happened to you and actually use it for good and turn it into a new mission.

"When I met Jason, I was still searching within myself. After I left WWE, I had a similar type of identity crisis for about two and a half years. I didn't know what I was going to do next. I was searching for my next thing. So meeting Jason at Cherrybend was perfect timing because he got me thinking about what my identity after wrestling might be. I saw his new mission in life and I wanted a new mission too.

"Soon after that I became a motivational speaker because I wanted to empower people because that's what Jason did for me.

"One of the main things I speak about now is identity. Knowing who you are, what you do, what your mission is, having a clear vision statement for your life and what you want to accomplish, and then having a clear plan to get there.

"It helps you to find what true success is. In my opinion, Jason Koger is the truest definition of success there is. All his accomplishments are super cool, and all the 'first person in the world' stuff he's done is awesome, but his character is so much more attractive. What a reward that is! If I can acquire that kind of character, that's the fruit that I'll leave behind for my children.

"Watching Jason sit around the fire with the soldiers at Cherrybend was really remarkable to see because these wounded warriors don't want to open up to just anybody off the street. They want to talk to people that have been through it like they have. So even though Jason's never been to battle, there is still this really cool connectivity that Jason has with these guys. You can see it when you're around them and you realize how they pick on each other and their inside jokes only they can make. That's where Jason's gentle spirit takes over. Not only does he have a common experience as an amputee, but he also has this magnetic personality and is just so down to earth that anyone feels comfortable talking to him.

"Cherrybend ends with a benefit concert on the last night. There's a moment I remember very clearly where Jason was letting these kids come up and see his arms. Kids are curious, you know. So, he's doing tricks with his arms and making them laugh, letting them touch his arms, and probably telling them silly jokes, but also leaving them with an encouraging word. He's always so present to whoever he is in front of at the time, whether it's a wounded warrior, another amputee, a celebrity, the ranch owner whose property we took the soldiers hunting on that week, or whoever. But then I turn around and he's cutting up with a group of kids. That was so Jesus-like to me. It reminded me of the scripture where Jesus says let the kids come to me.

"That's just another small example of turning his tragedy into a triumphant gift to the world."

I have met so many people at the events I've been to. At the next Handing Back event we have I'll get to invite my new friends to Owensboro and show them my town. My friends in Owensboro will also get to meet some celebrities who may have never had a reason to come to Owensboro before. Handing Back just naturally grows from year to year and all the money raised stays right here in Owensboro to help whoever needs it next. It's really fun.

I plan to invite some of my new hunting buddies to our next Handing Back, but that's a side story for the next chapter.

Handing Back is my way to repay that a little bit and pay it forward to someone else. It's one of my favorite things to do.

It's not about me. It's about using the opportunities God has given me to help somebody else. At the end of the day, I don't want to be known for having done a few TV shows or movies. I want to be known for giving back and helping others.

I'd love to be famous for that!

CHAPTER 14

HUNTING SHOWS AND MORE

"I went to hunting trade shows anyway and I would still go to them if I never had my accident. But now that I'm a double bilateral amputee, these hunting stars notice me."
~JASON

God can open doors for us, especially if we make ourselves available. I think that's true for everyone. Not just me. That's the only way I can explain everything that's happened the past 14 years since losing my arms, because there's no way in the world I could have designed this all on my own.

My number one goal is helping other people be successful and to show others that there is a God who will do some big, big things in your life—if you allow Him to. That's what's most important to me.

All these things—the TV shows, the magazine articles, all those things—are just more ways for my story to get out there so I can inspire other people AND help give other amputees hope. That's what this is all about. That's what I really care about the most.

This chapter is about how that passion and my other passion for hunting overlapped and opened up even more doors.

For years I've been going to the National Wild Turkey Federation convention in Nashville. Even before my accident. But

not long after my accident, I went by the Realtree booth because I always wanted to meet David Blanton, who is the vice president of Realtree. From what I've read about him, David seems to be a Christian and a really good dude. (*Realtree Outdoors* is an outdoors hunting show on the Outdoor Channel.)

The first year after I was hurt, I went to the Realtree booth and waited in line to meet David. At those conventions, David takes time to talk with everybody. So, as soon as I walked up, we said hi and started talking and he said to me, "I want to know your story." I gave him the real quick basics, but I felt horrible because there was probably a 30-minute line of people behind me. I told him my story the best I could in a minute and a half and gave him my card with my website and contact information on it.

I walked away happy that I got to meet David Blanton but didn't think anything else about it because he meets hundreds

of people at these conventions. There's no way he's going to remember me.

But the next year at NWTF I took a friend of mine and saw David again in the booth. He was standing there with Lee and Tiffany Lakosky, who had just become very popular as the hosts of *The Crush* TV show on the Outdoor Channel, so with the three of them standing there together the line was really, really long.

My friend and I decided not to stand in that long line and just walked on by them. But as we were walking by, I heard, "Jason, what are you doing?" I looked over my shoulder to see who was yelling and it was David. I started looking around, all confused, because I still didn't realize he was talking to me. I thought maybe there happened to be another person named Jason he was talking to.

But sure enough, he looked right at me and said, "I'm talking to you, Jason. Come over here."

They brought me and my friend around to the back of the booth without waiting in line. Well, David introduced me to Lee and Tiffany and told them about what happened to me. I was blown away that he not only remembered my name but remembered my story too. Then he said he wanted me to meet his son.

Ever since then, it's just sort of grown from there. I've been to Realtree in Georgia. David sent me some Realtree stuff to wear when I give speeches. I've got his cell number and we'll talk every once in a while.

After that second time meeting David at NWTF, it spread from there. I went to an Archery Trade Association show and reconnected with Lee and Tiffany. I ended up meeting Travis Turner, "T-Bone" on *Bone Collector*, too.

One day my phone rang and it popped up a number from Iowa. I thought it was a junk call. Who's going to call me from Iowa? But the voice on the other end says, "Hey, this is Tiffany Lakosky." I thought it was bullcrap. Somebody's pranking me. No way Tiffany Lakosky is calling me. She hunts with Brantley Gilbert, Luke Bryan, Rascal Flatts, lots of guys at a whole different level.

But it was really her. She went on to tell me that she had a friend whom she went to high school with who'd just lost an arm and I was the first person she thought of. She asked me if I would reach out to him and help him out. The reason she called was to see if she could pass on my number. Ever since then, we'll still text every now and then. Just this past fall she killed a huge elk and texted me a photo of it.

Things like that still blow me away. She hunts with all these famous people, but she still takes the time to text me. I just think that's so cool.

It's all because of my story. I think it comes down to people being impressed by my story.

I'm humbled so much that I've ended up meeting some of these people. It's because I'm different and I stand out in their memory. If I didn't stand out, then David Blanton would have walked past me the first time I met him and none of these hunting connections would have ever happened.

With Lee and Tiffany, it's same thing. There's no way they can remember all the hundreds or thousands of fans they meet at these big conventions and trade shows. But they remember a guy with no arms who still hunts. Now when I see them at these trade shows, they'll pull me aside with an hour-long line of people to meet and give me a hug and go on.

It's the same thing with the hunting show *Buck Commander* now too. Tombo Martin is one of the Buck Commander guys whom I became really good friends with and he introduced me to Adam Laroche. Most people know Adam from his time in major league baseball, but he hangs out with the Buck Commander guys now. He's the one who basically quit baseball because they wouldn't let his son come in the locker room with him during practice. He said his son was more important than the money. When he heard my story, he said, "I want you to come to my hometown and tell your story."

Obviously, it's the fact that I don't have hands that makes me stand out in these people's minds. At least initially. But I'd like to think that having fake arms might turn their head, but it's more because I'm a humble, genuine guy that I stand out. Or maybe because I'm not asking anything from them. Except to help me share my story to inspire other people. Maybe it's a combination of things.

Whatever it is, I truly feel like this is what God wants me to do.

He wants me to share my story and he's opening these doors for me so other people can help me share it too. Those same celebrities started out somewhere and had other people help them in the beginning. That's true for everybody. I'm so appreciative and humbled by that.

HUNTING SHOWS

"I believe that having an attitude of gratitude like Jason is critical in our quest for happiness."
~JANA WALLER

The same thing happened with Janna Waller, who is the host and producer of *Skull Bound Chronicles* on Carbon TV.

Me and Janna Waller

Again, I was walking through NWTF with my "Look Ma, No Hands" shirt on. Jana saw me walking by and pulled me aside and said, "Hey, I've got to know your story." That shirt is always a good conversation starter. When I quickly told her my story, she said, "I need your number."

She either called or emailed me the next day and asked me if she could do an article about me. She freelances for several hunting magazines. So, we did the interview, and then she invited me to come up and go on a hunt with her up in Illinois that would be filmed for Skull Bound TV. That was the first time I was ever on camera for a hunting show.

Jana shares the story:

"From the moment I saw Jason walk by in that T-shirt, I knew he must have a great outlook on life and I had to meet him. We got to talking and I was so impressed with his positive outlook. We stayed in touch, became good friends, and went on a whitetail hunt the following year.

"Jason is one of the happiest, most positive people I know. He has taken the tragedy of losing his hands and turned it into a story of triumph and perseverance that I believe the entire world can learn from.

"Jason's story is inspiring because every single person can relate to life throwing them challenges. Jason refused to let his tragedy define him as a victim but instead uses it to show others that nothing can deter you if you have a strong, positive attitude and grit.

"All of us deal with challenges and hard times, but when you truly put yourself in his shoes, you realize that so much in life is attitude and perspective, which I think is the key to success. People can choose to feel sorry for themselves and become victims of circumstance, or they can take their road bumps or tragedies and turn them into a story of true grit and triumph.

"We often take our health, in all aspects, for granted. I believe that having an attitude of gratitude like Jason does is critical in our quest for happiness. Jason's story makes me appreciate my life and the ease in which I live it. Whenever I'm dealing with a tough situation or having a bad day, stories like Jason's make me realize that I have nothing to complain about.

"While I feel many others in his position would have simply given up on life, Jason has grabbed the proverbial bull by the robotic hands and never looked back."

The timeline gets a little fuzzy in my mind, but that hunt with Jana was right around the time I was on *Hawaii Five-O*. I'm not sure which was first.

I was not successful on that hunt, but Jana and I became good friends. Since then she's gotten me involved with other connections she has in the hunting industry. It was a fun hunt for sure. It was hot though, I remember that!

One time after NWTF I was eating at a restaurant when one of the wives at a table with two couples next to us asked what happened to me. I stopped by their table and talked for a little while. She asked me if I was going to the NWTF show the next day and told me to stop by their booth. That booth ended up being a big outfitter in Kansas. I've always wanted to hunt in Kansas, so I was excited to meet them.

That was Beth Knight, who with her husband Mark Knight owns a hunting lodge called Midwest Whitetail Adventures out in Kansas. Mark invited me up there to come hunt at his lodge. Of course, I was not about to turn that down, so I went to Kansas and hunted with Mark and spent a week with them. Ever since then, I've almost been like family to them and I go up there whenever I can to hunt.

Not long after that, Mark started a hunting show called *Dirt Road Outdoors* and invited me out for a bear hunt. That's how I became the first bilateral amputee in the world to kill a bear with a crossbow.

When the bear hunt kill happened, there were several articles about it. I was in *Bear* magazine and another crossbow magazine that I know of.

Last year I killed a state record deer with my buddy Jeff Jacobs and his son, Zachary, on their land in Edmonson County. I was in a few more magazines after that, which was a lot of fun too. I had done a speech for Jeff in Edmonson County, so when he found out I liked to hunt, he invited me to come hunt with him and his son on this farm they were leasing. He sent me a picture of this deer they had seen there that ended up being a 184-inch deer. There's no telling how much money people might pay on a guided hunt to kill a deer like that! But Jeff had already filled his tags for the year, and so had his son. They both had seen that monster buck, but neither could get a good shot at him. At the end of the year, he took me to try and get it, and it just worked out for me.

I really want to stress that point about Jeff, because people who may not be familiar with hunting may not realize how big of a deal that was. Most people would keep a deer that big a secret and not tell anybody about it until they got to shoot it themselves. Even if it took years. But Jeff wanted to take me to see if I could kill it. It says a lot about the kind of person Jeff is that he gave me that opportunity. I was happy that I could harvest it on his land. But he was even happier to see me shoot it. I can't tell that story without giving proper thanks to Jeff Jacobs. He and I have become good friends since then.

Jeff tells the story:

"I wouldn't change a thing about the way it happened.

"I met Jason at an outdoor show up in Owensboro. I'm on the Chamber of Commerce in our town and we needed a guest speaker for our dinner, so I called Jason and he said he'd be glad to come speak to our group. I told him to come up early so I could show him my hunting spots. He thought that sounded good, so that's what we did.

"I took him out and started telling him about this giant deer on our land. It was easily a Boone and Crockett (trophy) deer. I told him about how I had pulled the trigger on it about 12 yards away on a Saturday morning in gun season but my bullet didn't fire. All it did was put a dent in the primer. That darn deer ran away before I could get another bullet loaded and fired. That was a heartbreaker! That would have been my biggest deer for sure.

"When I got down and picked the bullet up off the ground I could see where it put a dent in the primer and I took that bullet with me because I knew nobody would believe me. I dry fired the gun a few times and figured out what happened. There was a little spot of rust on the firing pin from where I was out in the rain the day before.

"I sat there a couple more hours and finally another buck came out and I shot that one and killed it so I was done for the season.

Me with Jeff Jacobs and our trophy deer

"I told Jason that story and he said it was the craziest thing he'd ever heard. We went to the dinner that night and he gave his speech, which is always moving for people. Then at the end of the night, I asked him if he wanted to come hunt that deer since I was tagged out.

"He thought I was kidding at first, but I told him I was serious.

"He came up a few times and we'd hunt that deer in the hot, dry, cold, wet, all different conditions. And we got to know each other a little better in the process too.

"We use those wireless trail cameras and they would always see that big buck come out about dusk. Never in the daytime. So that day we stayed out later, and all at once all these deer started walking out into the field and we noticed a couple bucks coming out. I looked through the binoculars and I told Jason, 'Oh, there he is! He's out there!'

"Sure enough, Jason ended up shooting it and I got it all on video. When you watch that video, I think I was more excited than he was.

"It was the last light of the last day of hunting season. What are the odds of that?

"My son was watching it all from another stand right around the corner of the field. He had already basically gotten bored with the hunt and was shooting at birds. So my kid's hunting in a stand 150 feet from us shooting at birds with an air rifle and we shoot a 184-inch buck! I love that because I tell people that you can have fun. It doesn't always have to be that serious or that competitive all the time.

"To be really honest, a lot of people that hunt around me weren't very happy that I took Jason out to hunt that big buck. Which made me think that maybe those guys ought not to be on my friend list if they're thinking that way.

"The way I see it, there's nobody that deserved that deer more than Jason because he was having a lot of bad days when you and I were having good days.

"I hope it opened up the eyes of some other people that there's just as much excitement and joy in seeing someone else get a trophy buck like that than there is in shooting one yourself.

"We've become very good friends since that day. We talk on the phone almost every day and we've been on trips together and everything. I still believe there's a reason all that happened.

"We've had some fun. And that's what it's all about. Since then, I've taken Jason back to that same field and he shot another big one! It's the craziest thing. He's got to be one of the luckiest hunters I've ever seen in my life.

"We also go to archery trade shows together. My son goes along with us, and anybody who's anybody in the outdoor world knows who Jason is. They're constantly coming up to him and saying hi and asking how he's doing.

"Here's another funny story I like to tell. Last year we were at the Archery Trade Association show, and as part of it they give you all kinds of free stuff from all the vendors and dealers. Shirts, stickers, scopes, and all kinds of hunting gear and products. I'm sure it's several hundred dollars' worth of stuff. After we got back to the hotel that night we dumped all the stuff out on the bed to see what we got because we were going to split it all up, between me, my son, and Jason. Jason starts digging through all this stuff like he's digging for gold and the thing he picked up and got all excited about was a cheap pair of fingernail clippers that had this big round disc on the back of it with an emblem on it.

"Without even thinking about it, I just said, 'Jason, what the heck are you going to do with those?'

"And he said, 'Here, I'll show you!' And he sat on the bed, took off his shoes, and used it to get to his toenails because he could hold on to it with that big old round emblem thing. We just laughed so hard because it was the funniest thing the way that happened, seeing him dig through that mountain of cool stuff and coming up with a pair of fingernail clippers.

"We put that picture on Facebook and it got a lot of comments.

"It is amazing what he can do. There would be days it was so cold outside when we were hunting. Single digits sometimes. And I'm telling you Jason can put on four layers of clothes as fast as me or you. That's pretty impressive.

"One time we were playing Monopoly and I'm not kidding, his stacks of play money were neater than mine. How he can take his hooks and grab that tiny, thin money is unbelievable. I had a hard time keeping up with where my little guy was on the board because I was mesmerized watching Jason play. So, it's no surprise to me that they say he's the number one bilateral upper limb prostheses user in the world."

From there, I went on another hunt in Kansas with Mark Knight. I didn't know this was going to happen, but when I got there, Jon and Gina Brunson from *Addicted to the Outdoors* were there, too. I was staying at a house with Mark that John and Gina were staying at too. As we were there, Jon mentioned, "Man, this would be an amazing story. Why don't I send my cameraman with Jason and I'll film myself and send the other cameraman to go along with Gina." We hunted that week and that is how I was on *Addicted to the Outdoors* because it just worked out that we were in Kansas at the same time.

Most of those hunting connections and opportunities that I just mentioned all came from that one happenstance connection at NWTF in Nashville.

It's funny how all those hunting shows came about. It was fun to be on those shows, but that's not the road for me. I couldn't do that full time and be out on hunts for weeks at a time away from the family. I don't think I'd want that life. I do enjoy hunting when I can. But I couldn't do it full time. I'm on the road enough for appointments and speaking engagements as it is.

THE UNITED ASSOCIATION OF PLUMBERS AND PIPEFITTERS

"All the UA speeches I've done are basically because of Brotherhood Outdoors."

~JASON

Brotherhood Outdoors is a TV show that features selected union members as they go on the hunt of a lifetime. Any union member can put in for a hunt and if you get selected, they'll take you out and film it.

I had already met the host of *Brotherhood Outdoors* at NWTF. He told me that I should put in for a hunt. About two years later, somehow my name popped up again. So, they reached out to me.

The president of the UA, Mark McManus, isn't a hunter, but he's on the board of *Brotherhood Outdoors*. That's how he heard my story, because of that episode of the show. All the UA speeches I've done are basically because of *Brotherhood Outdoors*.

Since that show aired, the UA has brought me into Louisville, KY, Colorado, and Las Vegas. I attended their national conference in 2021. Plus, I've been featured in the UA journal two or three times, which is really cool.

There's a lady named Brenda who works for the UA as a writer. She heard about my story and wanted to do an article for the UA journal. She wrote a really nice, two-to-three-page story about me. After it was published, she continued following me pretty closely.

Well, somebody called me and told me that Brenda's son was in a four-wheeler accident and lost his hand. I got her phone number from the UA and called her while her son was still in the hospital. We talked for a while on the phone and she told me, "You have no idea how much that means to me because as soon as I found out that my son lost his hand you were the first person I thought of."

It's all because she wrote that article about me. I think that's a connection that could only happen through God. He knew all this had happened to me and was going to happen to Brenda's son and He brought us all together through this article. I just think that's so cool.

There are so many companies that have helped me out now. Some of them send me things from time to time and some are basically sponsoring me. One person, for instance, is Bruce Swearingen, the owner of 4S Advance Wildlife Solutions, who sends me products to help with the deer herd.

One of these days, I'd love to hunt with Mike Miller the Turkey Killer because he seems to be such a down-to-earth, cool guy. He knows his stuff about turkey hunting and I think it would be a blast. That's one hunt that's still on my "bucket list" for one of these days.

AMBASSADOR FOR OTHER AMPUTEES

"Helping people is what I love to do."
~JASON

It's crazy how all these little circles connect and intersect in the hunting world. The UA, the acting appearances, the speaking engagements, even the ambassador programs for my prostheses. All of it ties in together and one builds on the rest. It's really neat to see.

I mentioned this before, but I'm an ambassador for Össur and Arm Dynamics. Plus, I get to meet other amputees because Össur flies me around the country to meet with them. I help and give them advice. Plus, I show them how to get a proper fit and what you are capable of when you do have a proper fit. It makes all the difference in the world.

I'm incredibly blessed to have that opportunity. I love talking with other amputees and helping them be successful. I'll have other amputees call me and when I call them back, they say things like, "Man, I can't believe you called me." Or they'll apologize and say, "I don't want to take much of your time." But I tell them, "Don't apologize, this is what I love to do!" I want to help other people. That's why I do what I do.

I try to be easy to get a hold of and even easier to talk to. When a new amputee googles upper limb amputee, I want to be the first person they find. Plus, I want them to be able to reach out to me because the earlier I can talk with them the faster I can help them.

My goal is to be the number one upper limb amputee when it comes to helping other amputees. I'm more than willing to help them out. I want them to succeed. I want to be that hope for them. That's why I want to be at the top.

These are examples of how everything I do is connected in some way. The fact that one thing leads to another and then another helped me realize that God wants me to share my story. It's Him saying, "Hey, Jason. You've got a story to tell that people need to hear."

I have no idea where it's all going to go or where it will end. I'm leaving that up to God too. But I do feel like the connections will keep coming together.

CHAPTER 15

TEDx EVANSVILLE

*"I'm very humbled that people keep asking me to come
share my story and feel blessed to be able to do what I do."*
~JASON

I'm very humbled that people keep asking me to come share my story and feel very blessed to be able to do what I do. It's really cool because I feel like I'm giving back and helping people realize their potential whether it's a motivational speech or if I'm talking to an amputee.

It feels good to have people interested in my story. Every week I'm getting calls to either come speak somewhere or talk with another amputee. It's really awesome to think that I'm getting these invitations and opportunities to share my story because it could help somebody else or change their life. That's become my purpose in life now.

I would have never imagined that.

That's why I was so excited when I got asked to do TEDx because I knew it could make me better as a speaker and take things to the next level. I always thought TEDx was for bigger cities like New York or LA. I never knew we had a regional TEDx close to us. When I was invited to speak at TEDx Evansville (Indiana), only 45 minutes away, I was surprised.

I knew what TEDx was but I didn't know how the process worked. I didn't realize you had to interview and audition and be picked.

Photo by Jordan Barclay Photography

When they called me and told me I had an interview, I didn't know what to expect at all. I showed up completely unprepared. I thought you just gave them an idea and explained what you were going to talk about, not actually give your talk.

I went in there thinking I was going to talk about my accident and everything that's happened since. Instead, I walked in there and they basically said, "All right, you have ten minutes to give your presentation. Go."

So, I just winged it.

I drove home feeling like I screwed up big-time. Even though I thought I did terrible, the lady called me back and told me they wanted to have me for the next TEDx Evansville.

I found out later that all the coaches listen to all the speeches and then they get together to decide who wants to work with which speaker. Apparently, I had two coaches who wanted to work with me so they decided to let two of them coach me. The first time we met, I went through my story and we talked about some ideas of what I wanted to do with it.

Photo by Jordan Barclay Photography

I explained to them it's much easier for me to talk 45 minutes or an hour than it is for 12 to 15 minutes because I know the points I want to make and the order of things. That's because I've done it so many times. After giving my full presentation to them, they helped me carve it down to a 15-minute window.

TEDx had started to promote on social media and I noticed they were using a picture of me for the promos. It was a shot with my arms crossed and it had the date of the TEDx live event. They rotated all the speakers on those ads. But when the ad with my picture was up, it got pretty good attention with shares and comments. Then I felt even worse, like, "Good Lord, I've totally fooled these people. They're going to be highly disappointed." That felt like a whole lot more pressure was on me.

After I worked on it for a while, I gave the trimmed-down version to the lady who was working on the program. She looked at me and said, "Wow. You need a book!" I told her, "Well, it's funny you say that because I'm actually working on a book right now." I wanted her to be honest too, just like my coaches were.

She was really excited about it and said it had the potential to go viral online.

By the night of the event, I felt really comfortable with the 15-minute talk because I had gone over it so many times and practiced it a lot. Every chance I got; I was going over it in my head. I felt ready.

I got to the event about two hours early to get prepared like they asked us to. They had all of us come out to the stage and stand in a circle and the host led us in this guided meditation with soothing music and breathing exercises. To help us relax, the host said, "Okay, I want everybody to close your eyes and touch your nose with your thumb and your first finger."

I opened my eyes a little and started chuckling. She had her eyes closed, too, so she cracked her eye open a little and looked over at me to see what I was laughing at. I couldn't help it. I just started busting up laughing. By that time, everybody had opened their eyes to see what I was laughing at, and she asked, "What's wrong?"

I tried to stop laughing enough just to say, "I'm sorry. But you're killing me!" Everybody laughed so hard and she got to laughing, too. I guess that helped break the ice for everybody.

Later on in the green room, we were all just hanging out before the event and cutting up with each other. I was talking with some people and the guy who heads the whole thing walked up to me and said, "Man, you're so chill. You're the most relaxed of anybody here. You aren't worried about this at all."

For some reason, they scheduled my talk second to last. When I wasn't going over my speech in my head, I would go up and peek out to the stage and watch some of the other speakers a while. All these other speakers kept on saying, "I can't wait till you go." So there again, I'm thinking, *Oh man, I got these people fooled too. I'm going to disappoint everybody.*

Finally, it was my turn, and right after I got off the stage the guy who was keeping time and lining us up to keep things moving came up to me and told me, "Dude, that was unbelievable." That surprised me because he heard every talk.

Come to find out, that guy does his own motivational program and is filming a documentary about how people can inspire others. His dad had cancer and would still work out every day. He told me his dad would flip a tire over and over all through his cancer treatments and it became a really inspirational thing for a lot of people who followed him through that process. After his dad passed, he kept his tradition going by flipping that tire to honor other cancer patients. That documentary is in honor of his father and he wants to include other stories too. He asked if I would be a part of it. We'll be working on that soon.

There have been some other neat things that have happened since TEDx. There was another guy who is a full-time motivational speaker and he invited me to this networking group that meets together every now and then.

I've been contacted a few times by people who were there or have seen my TEDx talk online. Two college students from Evansville who are doing a final project interviewed me.

In the fall of 2021, I was also featured in a book titled *Surrounded By Champions* by author Karen Hunsanger. She dedicated a whole chapter to my story and did a fantastic job. Because she feels my story is so inspirational, she offered to help me with this book too.

Overall, my first TEDx talk went better than I could have imagined. Working with those speech coaches was a great experience. I learned some little tips here and there from the other speakers too. It's always neat to learn from other people who do what you do.

Photo by Nicky Kessinger Photography

Photo by DJ Photography

CHAPTER 16

TODAY

*"Jason says he wouldn't change this. He
says he wouldn't go back, even if he could,
because he has a greater purpose now."*
~Jenny Koger

Up until COVID hit, our lives were pretty fast-paced. To be honest, the downtime probably did us some good. I should probably take care of myself better and not be so ambitious sometimes.

Just like the other night. I was cleaning the garage and I had a tote that I put a bunch of old trophies and things in that I wanted to store up in the attic. I told Jenny I needed her to help me. She was going to but the phone rang and she had to take the girls somewhere. Then I was left out in the garage with this heavy tote by myself. I'm hard-headed and impatient sometimes, so I just decided I was going to get it up there anyway.

I picked that heavy tote up with my hooks the best I could, but it kept sliding. I threw my arms off and tried it again with my residuals. With one residual underneath the tote and the other one to steady it, I started my way up the ladder with that heavy tote like a big dummy.

About halfway up that ladder, I got stuck and was about to fall. I couldn't go up any higher and couldn't go back down either without letting go of the tote and hoping it wouldn't knock me off the ladder. I didn't have any choice but to keep going. My arm and my back were hurting. It was not the smartest thing I've ever done. But I was already committed at that point.

I just told myself to take one more step. Take a break. One more step. Another break.

Finally, I got to the point where I could put the tote on top of my head and push it up over the lip of the attic. Then I climbed the rest of the way up and slid it over out of the way where it needed to go. All because I was stubborn.

But I wanted to complete the job. I didn't want to quit, and I was not going to let that tote go and drop it while watching everything inside get busted up.

Then another time recently, Jenny and I took carpet out of our house and this guy told me he'd come over to help me. He was going to cut it up in strips and take it out that way. But again, I got impatient, so Jenny and I took it out ourselves.

We rolled the whole thing up. Carpet and pad and everything. I told Jenny, "I think we can do it." Jenny got on one end, I got on one end, and we got it out the front door and laid it on the porch. By that time, I was worn out. The next day I was home by myself and it got on my nerves because it looked bad on the front porch. I got determined and dragged it over to the trailer. My neighbor brought his tractor over to lift it up into the trailer so we could haul it off.

Being that bullheaded all the time is going to catch up with me eventually. I'll probably have a bad back sooner than I should. That stubborn determination all goes back to the way I was raised and watching my mom and dad work hard to be successful. I'm the same way. Quitting is not an option.

Anyway, like I was saying, things the last year or two have fallen into a pretty good rhythm. Until the pandemic hit, I was doing regular speaking engagements and traveling quite a bit visiting other amputees. With the COVID shutdown, I lost several months' worth of events. Now finally they're picking back up again.

Just last week I spoke at a Kiwanis meeting in Bowling Green, Kentucky, which is about an hour away from our house, between Owensboro and Nashville. It was a small gathering, still socially distant, but I made some really good connections. One guy was from the local news station and invited me to come on the air soon to share my story in a segment. Another lady was from the local library and she said as soon as this book is out they'd have me down for a book signing at the library. Those two connections right there could open up a whole new market for me. Who knows what God could do from there?

Like a lot of other families, Jenny and I enjoyed spending more time at home with the kids during quarantine. As things slowly opened back up, the kids were starting to have practices and games again toward the end of the summer.

Jenny and I keep a pretty good balance, but we do have to work on it now that we have three kids going different directions with ball practice and everything else. When Axell was younger, he used to race dirt bikes, which was pretty fun, but that got to be too much. It's hard on Jenny loading dirt bikes in and out of the truck. When they tear up, Jenny can't fix them.

The girls both play softball. Every weekend I would take Axell racing and Jenny would take the girls to softball tournaments. What ended up happening, though, was I never saw the girls play and Jenny never got to see Axell race. Finally, after a year and a half of racing, we just decided it wasn't good for our family. We were tired of being split with way too many things going on. It wasn't fair for any of us.

The year before the pandemic, we got Axell into baseball

instead because it's much easier to divide up between baseball and softball and make it work. Whatever we do on the weekends, we want to do as a family.

With three kids, I can't just go hunting every time I want, but we talk about it and figure it out together. When I'm traveling for different events and speaking engagements, my mom helps Jenny a lot with the kids, and so does Jenny's mom. We have to work at it a little more to get it all done. But we do.

Jenny would tell you that we have a good, happy homelife. Sure, we argue sometimes, just like any couple, but we get along better now than we ever have.

I try to think ahead and make things easier for Jenny whenever I can. I've learned some little tricks, like if we're at a restaurant I'll just ask the server to have the cook cut up my entree for me so Jenny doesn't have to at the table.

We've been married 17 years this year. That happened in our third year of marriage. We made it through those tough years by working together and this is just normal for us now.

ALWAYS KEEP SMILING

"Toby and Holly are the ones that gave me the 'Look Ma, No Hands' shirt I'm always wearing."
~ JASON

Another aspect of our lives is we keep each other laughing. Every now and then someone will ask Jenny to come give a talk. Jenny and I were giving a talk together once, and I could tell she was nervous.

Right as they were introducing us, Jenny said her heart was

pounding and she whispered to me that her hands were sweating. Just to break the tension, I started by saying, "Jenny just leaned over and asked me if my hands were sweating as much as hers. Nope. I don't have that problem anymore."

Another time we were on vacation and my parents were with us. I was trying to kneeboard behind the boat. My dad was next to me helping me get situated on the kneeboard. At one point he grabbed a hold of the top of my arm up by the shoulder, and without even thinking I yelled, "Careful, Dad! Don't pull my *whole* arm off!"

I laughed so hard, but my dad just shook his head and said, "Oh my goodness! You didn't have to say *that!*"

Dad continues the story:

"He still got up on that kneeboard though! And that's the thing: he still does all these things anyway. There are a lot of people with two arms that still can't kneeboard. And here he is just figuring it out to prove to himself he can.

"There were no TV crews there for that. This book wasn't even talked about at that time. He was just figuring that out for himself, not for anybody else to see.

"Another example of that is getting his CDL license. There were a lot of things we had to figure out that people just weren't used to doing or seeing. We had a company dump truck for big jobs that Jason used to drive. After his accident, Jason wanted to keep driving that truck, so once he was back to normal activities, he asked me to take him to get his CDL license renewed.

"I drove him to take his test and this state trooper told us that he'd never given the test to anybody that didn't have hands, just using their two hooks. So he kind of sat there for a second and thought about it.

"We were just waiting to see what he was going to say next.

We didn't know if that was the end of it, or if we'd have to come back another time, or what. Then finally he said, 'Well, we'll just go through it like I would anybody else. I don't know what else to do but treat it just like any other test.'

"So he sent Jason through the test, but that meant Jason had to back up to the end of the trailer, crank it up, and do all those steps by himself. Like everything else, Jason just worked his way through every single step that a normal person would have to go through for the entire test and completed all of it. Just like anybody else.

"He passed with no problem. That state trooper and I were both amazed. But not Jason. He was just like, 'Okay, what's next?'"

Dr. Guy still laughs about the first time I drove to Nashville by myself for a follow-up appointment. Dr. Guy asked where Jenny was and I told him she couldn't come this time so I just drove myself. He looked at me a little funny and said, "Jason, do you think you *should* be driving?" I didn't think anything about it. I just said, "Well, I've got my license, don't I?" Dr. Guy just laughed and said, "Well, yeah, I guess you do."

One of Toby's favorite stories is the time I got pulled over for speeding. We were on a family trip and Toby was following right behind me. Here's how Toby remembers it:

"The cop put his lights on, passed me up, pulled behind Jason, and walked up to Jason's window. I see Jason pass his license through the window with his hook. Jason and the cop end up having a nice, long conversation, I'm sure about his arms and his accident and whatever. I'm sure that cop had never seen a bilateral amputee driving his family on vacation before. We were going 75 in a 55, but next thing you know, the cop just gives him a warning and apparently tells him to be safe and lets him go.

"That's just Jason. He can talk his way out of anything.

"There's no stopping him. I remember on another vacation Jason was bound and determined he was going to get up on a kneeboard behind the boat just to prove that he could. Which is hard for people with two arms and two hands. He can't get out on the water with prostheses, obviously, which means he had to hook his nubs through the ski rope handle and bear-hug it the best he could to stay up. You or I would be white-knuckling it. It took him a few times, but he figured it out. Then it was off to the races from there!

"Things like that most people take for granted but seeing him out there riding waves behind a boat just like anybody else is just amazing. That's one of a thousand stories I could tell about things he's done and overcome."

LOOKING FORWARD, AND LOOKING UP ·

"I truly believe things happen for a reason."
~ JASON

At this point in my life, with the worst of COVID behind us, I'm looking forward to whatever God has in store for me next. More speaking gigs. Talking with more amputees. I can't wait to see what this book will lead to. I'm also looking forward to working on the next Handing Back event in Owensboro.

As soon as I can, I'll get back down to Vanderbilt to visit more patients. It doesn't bother me at all to go back to Vanderbilt when I volunteer. I don't get nervous walking back into the same hospital or the same floor or even the same room I was in.

I think it's because I truly believe that it all happened for a reason and I've been able to impact a lot of people who may never have had hope because of all this. That's why I do what I do.

In my mind, it was ultimately God who saved my life, but the whole team at Vandy had a role in that, and Dr. Guy was the one who had the knowledge and expertise to do what he had to do. The way that night was handled set me up to be able to do what I do today, both in my day-to-day living and in my calling to help other people. It all goes back to those decisions in the operating room.

Today, when I look back and think about all that, I can honestly say I'm happy with the way things turned out.

EXPECT GREATNESS

It took me years to realize God did answer my prayers—not how I was asking, but how He saw fit.
~Jenny Koger

People have a hard time believing me when I say I wouldn't change this, even if I could. It's because I have a greater purpose now.

Jenny feels the same way. As she puts it, "You don't realize how much you depend on God until things aren't perfect in your life." From Jenny's perspective, you can say you depend on God, and trust in God, but do you *really*?

I asked Jenny to share her final thoughts in this last chapter, so I'll leave you with this because I think Jenny describes it perfectly.

"I believe when you're put in situations like we were, God is totally transforming you. It doesn't happen overnight and you may not even notice it at the time.

"In the very beginning I said something really stupid like, 'God won't give you more than you can handle,' and after a while I sat there and thought, why did I say that? This is way more than I can handle. Way, way more. Maybe God gave me this so I would realize I'm not alone. Because we did get through this.

"I'm careful not to say things like that anymore because I don't want to sound misleading.

"But it took me years of growing and living in this new reality to come to that conclusion.

"It's Romans 8:28. Our kids know this verse. 'God works all things for the good of those who love Him.' All things. It's going to be okay. Whatever happens, it's going to be okay.

"I've changed so much through this experience.

"I grew up in church my whole entire life. I was baptized when I was eight years old. But my faith matured so much through this.

"I joke with Jason and wonder who would really want to read a book about our life. Because it's just normal to me. But the experience of working on this book has been so amazing to look back and see how God orchestrated it all.

"People question God a lot.

"It's normal to ask, 'Why me?' But when you know that God works all things for the good of those who love Him, your perspective is a little bit different. For me, that verse means that God wants to do something in your heart through the hard times. If you're looking for it going in, it's easier to see. That doesn't make it any easier; it's still hard going through it, but your perspective is different.

"It's one thing to read that God works all things for our good. It's another thing to really believe it. It's a whole other thing to live it.

"But because I knew that, I expected the good in the end. I

didn't know what it would be, but I expected it. I knew it wasn't going to be easy, but I never questioned the good at the end. I didn't know what it would be. I didn't know how long it would take us to get there. I couldn't have dreamt the struggles we've had along the way. But I never lost the end result that I knew would come.

"Our prayers aren't always answered the way we want them to be. Bad things do happen to good people. March 1, 2008, I prayed for a miracle. It took me years to realize God did answer my prayers—not how I was asking, but how He saw fit. In His perfect will. Generations in our family to come will tell this story of perseverance and God's faithfulness.

"God has worked this for our good, and for our family's good. Also for the good of a lot of other people through Jason sharing his story.

"Jason and I are grateful and humbled every day for the way we've been blessed through this. Again, that goes back to his parents and my parents raising us in church the way they did.

"Our hope is that this book has helped you see how God has worked all things for your good in your own life too. So I pray that as you read this you could feel God's goodness all through-out this book. Adversity is a reality, for everyone, but what it's not is permanent.

"I have a changed perspective now having gone through this. Struggles are inevitable—but I expect greatness! God has used our struggles, in His timing, for good.

"He has done it in the past so my faith assures me He will do it again.

"God loves me so much that He continues to work on my heart. He doesn't give up on me. And He won't give up on you.

"I want to share one last thought with you. I love music, it speaks to my heart in ways I can't explain. One song that repeatedly plays in my head is 'Fires' by Jordan St. Cyr. Listen to it! There's a verse in the song that really resonates with me . . .

I'll walk through these fires

Cause You're walking with me

I'm changed by Your mercy

Covered by Your peace

I'm living out the victory

Doesn't mean I won't feel the heat

"No pun intended, the heat of this burned us all—BUT that's not our ending! It's not yours either!

"I pray that you will change your perspective. Expect greatness from our God!

"'Now then, stand still and see this *great thing*

the Lord is about to do before your eyes.'

–1 Samuel 12:16."

NO
HANDS

"TO BE CONTINUED"

Jenny laughed when I told her I wanted to call the last little epilogue here, "To Be Continued" because she thought it meant there was going to be another book. Like a Part Two or something.

But that's not what I meant. I mean my story is still in progress.

With everything that's happened in the 14 years since losing my arms, I have no idea what God is going to do with my story in the next 14 years.

But it's going to be something special, I can tell you that!

As I'm writing this epilogue, I just got back from TK's Celebrity Softball Classic game in Texas that was postponed from COVID. We finally got to play it on June 12, 2021. That was a really fun weekend and it was great to be a part of something that raised money for two great organizations: Folds of Honor and Vets for Child Rescue. I was able to share my story with some people, and thanks to some attachments, I was able to throw and catch well enough to play in the outfield.

I met Michael Irvin and Zeke Elliott from the Dallas Cowboys, Gordie Gronkowski (Super Bowl champion Rob Gronkowksi's brother), Todd Chrisley from *Chrisley Knows Best*, actor Faizon Love from the movie *Elf*, Cody Jinks, who is probably the biggest independent country music artist in America right now, and rapper The D.O.C., who started out with NWA and Dr. Dre but lost his voice after being injured in a car accident. Hearing how he's found a new purpose since his injury was inspirational to me.

Every time I have a conversation like that it motivates me even more to use the opportunities God has given me.

Whatever happens, I want people to know that no matter how bad off you feel, or no matter what unforeseen circumstance life throws at you, you can always wake up in the morning with a smile on your face. You can go on living. There will be good that comes from it.

This book is meant to help you with your obstacles because each and every one of us will have obstacles to overcome throughout our lives. Some are bigger than others. Life is hard, but how we live through the hard times truly defines who we are. My story is something everyone can learn from. I am not perfect and I am not Superman. I just have faith.

I have heard thousands of times, "If I went through what you have, I don't think I could do what you have done."

You know what? You can.

You just have to find your faith. We were all born with faith. It's just that sometimes you have to dig a little deeper to find it. I have had some amazing opportunities and I am blessed that God opened those doors for me. If this book saves one person it is a success. If you don't know God, just look deeper because He is there.

God is not done with me, and He's not done with you.

So, get up, and get going. There's more to life than whatever dark time you find yourself in. I hope and pray you will find your greater purpose too.

ACKNOWLEDGMENTS

JASON KOGER

Writing this book has truly been a blessing! To look back on our journey as well as the many people that facilitated my success has been a humbling experience. First off, I want to say I serve an amazing God. Without Him none of this would have been possible. I know God placed the right people in my life at the exact right time. God placed the best doctors in my path, and God's hand was always guiding even if we couldn't see the plans. God never says he will not give us more than we can handle, but he does tell us in Mark 9:23, "If you believe, everything is possible for one who believes."

Danny May, thank you for the hours you put in to help share this story. Karen Hunsanger, thanks for helping rearrange the way it ended. Thanks to Curt Harding for doing the first edit, Tanner+West for the amazing book cover, and Carol Butler with Butler Books for publishing.

Next I want to thank my Mom and Dad for raising Holly and me to put God first and for giving us the resources we needed to succeed. I am blessed that God created the perfect wife for me, Jenny, and for getting to share our life with three amazing kids, Billie Grace, Cambell, and Axell. Family is the second most important thing in life behind my savior Jesus Christ. I am blessed to have my sister Holly, brothers-in-law Toby, Dave, and Michael, sisters-in-law Carrie and Tyler, and my in-laws Rhonda and Jeff. I was blessed to have met Jenny's dad before he passed away, and I know that if Billy were still around, we would have been building all kinds of things for my arms.

I also want to say thank you to all of our extended family and friends, too many to name, but I am grateful for each and every one. Thank you to Dr. Jeffery Guy and all of his staff. Their ability to rehabilitate, love, and care inspired and pushed me to overcome. Thankful for everyone involved at Arm Dynamics, Össur, Enhancing Skills For Life, Texas Assistive, Fillauer, and all involved with my technology. Also the members of the UA plumbers and pipefitters across the country.

Last, but not least, I want to thank YOU for reading my story and allowing me to share what God has done in my life. I hope you will follow my journey on social media or at www.jasonk-oger.com. I would absolutely love to hear your feedback on this book or to have the opportunity to speak to your group.

DANNY MAY

The power of story has always been my passion. So, first of all, thanks to Jason Koger for allowing me the privilege to help share your story with the world. You could have used any ghostwriter, but you chose a regular ol' guy from Owensboro (just like you). It's been an honor and this has been an amazing experience. Your story inspired me the first time we met for an Owensboro Living magazine article, and it continues to inspire me today.

Special thanks also to Karen Hunsanger, our developmental editor, for making this manuscript stronger and helping us "bring it back down the mountain." This is a much better book because of your dedication to it.

Carol Butler and the entire team at Butler Books are amazing to work with. I'm so glad we were able to keep the production of this book right here in Kentucky. You are masters of your craft who truly care for your authors and treat each project with care, respect, and pride. Thanks, Carol, for your professionalism and class.

To the design team at Tanner+West, thanks for making this cover look awesome.

Thanks also to my wife, Kelly, for her constant support and encouragement. You always make everything better.

Lastly and most importantly, all glory and honor belongs to God alone. Thank you, Lord.

I would like to express my thanks and appreciation
to the United Association of Plumbers and Pipefitters
for your constant support over the years.

I am proud to be a member of Local 633
Plumbers and Pipefitters Union.

ABOUT THE AUTHORS

JASON KOGER

Jason Koger became the first bilateral arm amputee in the world to be fitted with multi-articulating bionic hands after losing both hands in a traumatic ATV accident in 2008. Today, he encourages others to live a life without limitations.

When Jason is not at home helping his wife, Jenny, with their three children, Billie Grace, Cambell, and Axell, he is traveling the country sharing his story of overcoming obstacles or working as an ambassador for the manufacturer of his hands, Össur, and his socket manufacturer, Arm Dynamics.

With a positive attitude and welcoming personality, Jason has had the opportunity to appear on several national news outlets, which led to many other TV appearances, magazine articles, and the TEDx stage.

Jason has reached goals that have never been reached before, including becoming the first bilateral arm amputee to harvest a bear with a crossbow. Jason also started a charity event called Handing Back that has brought celebrities to his hometown of Owensboro, Kentucky, raising over $30,000 to give back to a community that gave so much to him in his time of need.

He recently received the American Red Cross Hero of the Year and Role Model of the Year awards.

Nobody knows what is next for Jason, but whatever doors open he will give the glory to God and grab every opportunity with both bionic hands.

DANNY MAY

Danny May is a freelance writer, author, and ghostwriter from Owensboro, Kentucky. He is a regular contributor to *Owensboro Parent* and *Owensboro Living* magazines and ghostwrote Earl Hayden's book *The First Family of Racing* in 2014.

KAREN HUNSANGER

Karen Hunsanger, contributor to *Handed a Greater Purpose* and author of *Surrounded by Champions*, is an enthusiastic fan of success stories, especially when the achiever has overcome extraordinary odds. Retired after a lengthy career in the corporate world and as an entrepreneur, she is passionate about using her experience to help others tell their stories as a ghostwriter and content editor. She also loves to hear from readers. Send her an email at karen@karenhunsanger.com or visit her website at www.karenhunsanger.com.

FOLLOW JASON

To learn more about Jason Koger, visit his website at www.jasonkoger.com and follow him on social media:

INSTAGRAM
@jkoger84

FACEBOOK
@jasonkogeroffical

TWITTER
@koger84

TIKTOK
@jason_koger